TRANSLATED

Translated Language Learning

The Diaries of Adam and Eve
アダムとイブの日記

Mark Twain
マークトウェイン

English /日本語

Copyright © 2023 Tranzlaty
All rights reserved.
Published by Tranzlaty
ISBN: 978-1-83566-187-1
Original texts by Mark Twain:
Extracts from Adam's Diary: Translated from the Original MS
First published in The Niagara Book 1893
Eve's Diary
First published in Harper's Bazaar 1905
Illustrated by Lester Ralph
www.tranzlaty.com

- Extracts from Adam's Diary -
-アダムの日記からの抜粋-

I had translated a portion of this diary some years ago
私は数年前にこの日記の一部を翻訳しました
a friend of mine printed a few copies of the text
私の友人がテキストのコピーを数部印刷しました
the text was in an incomplete form
テキストは不完全な形式でした
but the public never got to see those texts
しかし、一般の人々はそれらのテキストを見ることはありませんでした
Since then I have deciphered some more of Adam's hieroglyphics
それ以来、私はアダムの象形文字をもう少し解読しました
he has now become sufficiently important as a public character
彼は今や公のキャラクターとして十分に重要になっています
and I think this publication can now be justified
そして私はこの出版物が今正当化できると思います
- *Mark Twain*
- マークトウェイン

***

MONDAY - 月曜日
This new creature with the long hair is constantly in the way
長い髪のこの新しい生き物は常に邪魔をしています
It is always hanging around and following me about
それはいつもぶらぶらして私を追いかけています
I don't like this
このことを知りません
I am not used to company
私は会社に慣れていません
I wish it would stay with the other animals
他の動物と一緒にいてくれたらいいのにと思います

Cloudy to-day, wind in the east
今日は曇り、東の風
I think we shall have rain
雨が降ると思います
Where did I get that word?
どこでその言葉を手に入れましたか?
I remember now
私は今覚えています
the new creature uses that word
新しい生き物はその言葉を使います

TUESDAY - 火曜日
I've been examining the great waterfall
私は素晴らしい滝を調べてきました
the great waterfall is the finest thing on the estate, I think
素晴らしい滝は、敷地内で最高のものだと思います
The new creature calls it Niagara Falls
新しい生き物はそれをナイアガラの滝と呼んでいます
why does it call it Niagara falls?
なぜナイアガラの滝と呼ばれるのですか?
I am sure I do not know
私は知らないと確信しています
it says the waterfall looks like Niagara Falls
滝はナイアガラの滝のように見えると書かれています
That is not a reason
それは理由ではありません
it is mere waywardness and imbecility
それは単なるわがままと無礼です
I get no chance to name anything myself
自分で名前を付ける機会はありません
The new creature names everything that comes along
新しいクリーチャーは、付属するすべてのものに名前を付けます
I don't even get time to protest
抗議する時間すらありません
the same pretext is always offered

同じ口実が常に提供されます
"it looks like the thing"
「それは事のように見えます」
There is the dodo, for instance
たとえば、ドードーがあります
it says the moment one looks at it one sees the animal "looks like a dodo"
それを見た瞬間、動物は「ドードーのように見える」と書かれています
It will have to keep that name, no doubt
間違いなく、その名前を維持する必要があります
It wearies me to fret about it
それについて心配するのは私を疲れさせます
and it does no good to worry about it, anyway
とにかく、それについて心配するのは良くありません
Dodo! It looks no more like a dodo than I do
ドードー！それは私よりもドードーのようには見えません

WEDNESDAY - 水曜日

I built myself a shelter against the rain
私は雨に対する避難所を自分で建てました
but I could not have it to myself in peace
しかし、私はそれを安心して自分自身に持つことができませんでした
The new creature intruded
新しい生き物が侵入しました
I tried to put it out
出してみました
but it shed water out of the holes it looks with
しかし、それはそれが見える穴から水を流します
it wiped the water away with the back of its paws
それは足の後ろで水を拭き取りました
and it made a noise like the animals do when they are in distress
そして、動物が苦しんでいるときのように音を立てました
I wish it would not talk
話さないでほしい

it is always talking
それはいつも話しています
That sounds like a cheap fling at the poor creature
それは貧しい生き物への安い投げのように聞こえます
but I do not mean it to sound like a slur
しかし、私はそれがスラーのように聞こえるという意味ではありません
I have never heard the human voice before
私はこれまで人間の声を聞いたことがありません
for me it is a new and strange sound
私にとって、それは新しくて奇妙な音です
and this sound intrudes itself upon the solemn hush of these dreaming solitudes
そして、この音は、これらの夢を見る孤独の厳粛な静けさに侵入します
it offends my ear and seems a false note
それは私の耳を怒らせ、誤ったメモのようです
And this new sound is so close to me
そして、この新しい音は私にとても近いです
it is right at my shoulder, right at my ear
それは私の肩のすぐそば、私の耳のすぐそばにあります
first on one side and then on the other
最初は片側に、次に反対側に
I am used only to sounds that are at a distance from me
私は私から離れた音だけに慣れています

FRIDAY - 金曜日
The naming goes recklessly on, in spite of anything I can do
私ができることは何でもあるにもかかわらず、命名は無謀に続きます
I had a very good name for the estate: Garden of Eden
私はその地所にとても良い名前を持っていました：エデンの園
it was musical and pretty
それは音楽的できれいでした
Privately, I continue to call it that
個人的には、私はそれをそう呼び続けています
but I don't call it that in public anymore

しかし、私はもうそれを公の場では呼びません
The new creature says it is all woods and rocks and scenery
新しい生き物は、それがすべて森と岩と風景であると言います

therefore it has no resemblance to a garden, it says
したがって、それは庭に似ていない、とそれは言います
it says it looks like a park
公園のように見えると書かれています
it says it does not look like anything but a park
公園以外の何物にも見えないと書かれています
without consulting me, it decided to rename the garden
私に相談せずに、それは庭の名前を変更することに決めました
now it's called Niagara falls park
現在はナイアガラフォールズパークと呼ばれています
it is becoming too much for me
それは私には多すぎます
And there is already a sign up
そして、すでにサインアップがあります
"Keep off the grass"
「草に近づかないでください」
My life is not as happy as it was
私の人生は以前ほど幸せではありません

SATURDAY - 土曜日
The new creature eats too much fruit
新しい生き物は果物を食べすぎます
We may well run short of fruit quite soon
すぐに実がなくなるかもしれません
"we", again. That is one of its words
再び「私たち」。それはその言葉の一つです
I've heard the word so many times
私はその言葉を何度も聞いたことがあります
and now it's one of my words too
そして今、それも私の言葉の1つです

There is a good deal of fog this morning
今朝はかなり霧がかかっています
I do not go out in the fog
霧の中は出かけない
The new creature always goes out in the fog
新しい生き物はいつも霧の中に出かけます
It goes out in all weathers
それはすべての天候で消えます
it stumps around outside with its muddy feet and talks
泥だらけの足で外を歩き回り、話します
It used to be so pleasant and quiet here
ここはとても快適で静かでした

SUNDAY - 日曜日
This day is getting to be more and more trying
この日はますます挑戦的になっています
last November we made this day a day of rest
昨年11月、私たちはこの日を休息の日にしました
I already had six days of rest per week
私はすでに週に6日間の休息がありました
This morning I found the new creature at the forbidden tree
今朝、私は禁断の木で新しい生き物を見つけました
it was trying to clod apples out of that forbidden tree
それはその禁じられた木からリンゴを塊にしようとしていました

MONDAY - 月曜日
The new creature says its name is Eve
新しい生き物はその名前がイブだと言います
That is all right
それは大丈夫です
I have no objections to it being called Eve
私はそれがイブと呼ばれることに異議はありません
it says I should call Eve when I want it to come
それは私がそれをしたいときにイブに電話するべきだと言います
I said that would be superfluous

私はそれが不必要だと言った
The word evidently raised me in its respect
その言葉は明らかに私を尊敬の念を抱かせました
it is indeed a large and good word
それは確かに大きくて良い言葉です
this word will be worth repeating
この言葉は繰り返す価値があります
It says it is not an "it"
それはそれが「それ」ではないと言います
it says it is a "She"
それはそれが「彼女」であると言います
This is probably doubtful
これはおそらく疑わしいです
but it is all the same to me
しかし、それは私にとってすべて同じです
whatever she is wouldn't matter if she didn't talk so much
彼女がそんなに話さなければ、彼女が何であれ、問題ではありません

TUESDAY - 火曜日
She has littered the whole estate with execrable names and offensive signs:
彼女は不動産全体に実行可能な名前と不快な兆候を散らかしました:
"this way to the whirlpool"
「渦へのこの道」
"this way to goat island"
「ゴート島へのこの道」
"cave of the winds this way"
「風の洞窟はこちら」
She says this park would make a tidy summer resort
彼女は、この公園が整頓された夏のリゾートになると言います
but summer resorts are not at all customary
しかし、夏のリゾート地はまったく慣習的ではありません
"Summer resort" - another invention of hers
「サマーリゾート」 - 彼女のもう一つの発明

just words without any meaning
意味のないただの言葉
What is a summer resort?
避暑地とは?
But it is best not to ask her
しかし、彼女に尋ねないのが最善です
she has so much energy for explaining
彼女は説明するのにとても多くのエネルギーを持っています

FRIDAY - 金曜日
She has taken to beseeching me to stop going over the Falls
彼女は私に滝を越えるのをやめるように懇願しました
What harm does it do?
それはどんな害を及ぼしますか?
Says it makes her shudder
それは彼女を震えさせると言います
I wonder why it makes her shudder
なぜそれが彼女を震え上がらせるのだろうか
I have always jumped down from the waterfalls
私はいつも滝から飛び降りてきました
I liked the plunge and the excitement
私は飛び込みと興奮が好きでした
and I liked the coolness of the water
そして私は水の涼しさが好きでした
I supposed it was what the Falls were for
私はそれが滝の目的だと思いました
They have no other use that I can see
彼らは私が見ることができる他の用途はありません
and they must have been made for something
そして彼らは何かのために作られたに違いありません
She says they were only made for scenery
彼女はそれらが風景のためだけに作られたと言います
like the rhinoceros and the mastodon
サイやマストドンのように
I went over the Falls in a barrel
私は樽で滝を越えました
but that was not satisfactory to her

しかし、それは彼女にとって満足のいくものではありませんでした
I Went over the falls in a tub
私は浴槽で滝を越えて行きました
it was still not satisfactory
それでも満足のいくものではありませんでした
I swam the Whirlpool and the Rapids in a fig-leaf suit
私はイチジクの葉のスーツでワールプールとラピッズを泳ぎました
my suit got very damaged
私のスーツは非常に損傷しました
so I had to listen to tedious complaints about my extravagance
だから私は自分の贅沢についての退屈な不満に耳を傾けなければなりませんでした
I am too hampered here
私はここであまりにも妨げられています
What I need is change of scenery
必要なのは景色の変化

SATURDAY - 土曜日
I escaped last Tuesday night and travelled two days
私は先週の火曜日の夜に脱出し、2日間旅行しました
I built another shelter in a secluded place
私は人里離れた場所に別の避難所を建てました
and I obliterated my tracks as well as I could
そして私はできる限り自分の足跡を消しました
but she hunted me out with the aid of one of her beasts
しかし、彼女は獣の一人の助けを借りて私を追い出しました
a beast which she has tamed and calls a wolf
彼女が飼いならしてオオカミと呼ぶ獣
she came making that pitiful noise again
彼女は再びその哀れな音を立てて来ました
and she was shedding that water out of the places she looks with
そして彼女は彼女が見ている場所からその水を流していました

I was obliged to return with her
私は彼女と一緒に戻ることを余儀なくされました
but I will emigrate again, when an occasion presents itself
しかし、機会が現れたら、私は再び移住します

She engages herself in many foolish things
彼女は多くの愚かなことに従事しています
she's trying to understand why the lions and tigers eat grass and flowers
彼女はライオンとトラが草や花を食べる理由を理解しようとしています
she says their teeth would indicate that they were intended to eat each other
彼女は、彼らの歯は彼らがお互いを食べることを意図していたことを示していると言います
This is a foolish idea
これは愚かな考えです
to do that they would have to kill each other
そのためには、彼らはお互いを殺さなければならないでしょう
as I understand it that would introduce what is called "death"
私が理解しているように、それはいわゆる「死」を導入するでしょう
and I have been told that death has not yet entered the Park
そして私は死がまだ公園に入っていないと言われました
on some accounts that is a pity
いくつかのアカウントでそれは残念です

SUNDAY - rested
日曜日 - 休む

MONDAY - 月曜日
I believe I see what the week is for
私はその週が何のためにあるのかわかると信じています
it is to give time to rest up from the weariness of Sunday
日曜日の疲れから休む時間を与えることです

It seems a good idea
それは良い考えのようです

She has been climbing that tree again
彼女は再びその木に登っています
I clodded her out of it
私は彼女をそれからだましました
She said nobody was looking
彼女は誰も見ていないと言った
she seems to consider that a sufficient justification
彼女はそれを十分な正当化だと考えているようです
but it is no justification for chancing a dangerous thing
しかし、それは危険なことを偶然にすることを正当化するものではありません
I told her it was no justification for what she did
私は彼女に、それは彼女がしたことの正当化ではないと言いました
The word "justification" moved her admiration
「正当化」という言葉が彼女の賞賛を動かしました
she seemed to envy me a little, I thought
彼女は私を少しうらやましく思っているようだ、と私は思った
It is a good word
いい言葉です
I shall use the word more often
私はもっと頻繁にその言葉を使います

THURSDAY - 木曜日
She told me she was made out of one of my ribs
彼女は私の肋骨の1つから作られたと私に言いました
I somewhat doubt what she says
私は彼女の言うことをやや疑っています
I don't seem to be missing a rib
私は肋骨を見逃していないようです
and I can't imagine how she would have been made from my rib
そして、彼女が私の肋骨からどのように作られたか想像でき

ません
She is making a great fuss about the buzzard
彼女はノスリについて大騒ぎしています
she says his stomach does not agree with the grass
彼女は彼の胃が草と一致しないと言います
she is afraid she can't raise the buzzard
彼女はノスリを上げることができないのではないかと心配しています
she thinks it was intended to live on decayed flesh
彼女はそれが腐った肉で生きることを意図していたと思います
The buzzard must get along the best it can with what is provided
ノスリは、提供されているものでできる限りうまくやらなければなりません
We cannot overturn the whole scheme to accommodate the buzzard
ノスリに対応するための計画全体を覆すことはできません

SATURDAY - 土曜日
She fell in the pond while she was looking at herself in it
彼女は池の中で自分を見ている間に池に落ちました
she is always looking at herself
彼女はいつも自分自身を見ています
She was nearly strangled by the water
彼女はほとんど水に首を絞められていた
and she said it was most uncomfortable
そして彼女はそれが最も不快だと言った
This made her sorry for the creatures which live in the water
これは彼女を水中に住む生き物を気の毒に思いました
the creatures which she calls fish
彼女が魚と呼ぶ生き物
she continues to fasten names on to things that don't need them
彼女はそれらを必要としないものに名前を付け続けています
the don't come when they are called by those names
彼らがそれらの名前で呼ばれるとき、来ないでください

but this is a matter of no consequence to her
しかし、これは彼女にとって何の影響もありません
she is such a numbskull
彼女はとてもしびれた頭蓋骨です
she took a lot of the fish out of the water last night
彼女は昨夜、水からたくさんの魚を取り出しました
and then she brought them into the house
それから彼女は彼らを家に連れて行きました
she put them in my bed so they would be warm
彼女はそれらを私のベッドに置いたので、彼らは暖かくなります
but they don't seem any happier than where they were before
しかし、彼らは以前よりも幸せそうに見えません
all I can see is that they are quieter
私が見ることができるのは、彼らがより静かであることだけです
When night comes I shall throw them out again
夜が来たらまた捨てよう
I will not sleep with these fish in my bed again
私は二度と私のベッドでこれらの魚と一緒に寝ません
I find lying unclothed among them clammy and unpleasant
私は彼らの間で服を脱いで横たわっているのがベトベトで不快だと思います

SUNDAY - rested
日曜日 - 休む

TUESDAY - 火曜日
She has made friends with a snake
彼女はヘビと友達になりました
The other animals are glad that she is friends with the snake
他の動物は彼女がヘビと友達であることを嬉しく思います
because she was always experimenting with the other animals
彼女はいつも他の動物で実験していたからです
and she was always bothering the other animals

そして彼女はいつも他の動物を悩ませていました
and I am also glad she is friends with the snake
そして私は彼女がヘビと友達であることを嬉しく思います
because the snake talks
ヘビが話すので
now she spends more time talking with the snake instead of me
今、彼女は私の代わりにヘビと話すことにもっと時間を費やしています
and this enables me to get a rest
そして、これは私が休息をとることを可能にします

FRIDAY - 金曜日
She says the snake advises her to try the fruit of the forbidden tree
彼女は、ヘビが禁じられた木の実を試すように彼女に忠告すると言います
and she says the result will be a great and fine and noble education
そして彼女は、その結果は偉大で立派で高貴な教育になるだろうと言います
I told her there would be another result, too
私は彼女に、別の結果もあるだろうと言いました
eating from the tree would introduce death into the world
木から食べることは世界に死をもたらすでしょう
telling her the fruit would bring death into the world was a mistake
果物が世界に死をもたらすだろうと彼女に言うのは間違いでした
it would have been better to keep the remark to myself
その発言を自分に留めておいたほうがよかったでしょう
telling her about death gave her another idea
彼女に死について話すことは彼女に別の考えを与えました
she could save the sick buzzard
彼女は病気のノスリを救うことができました
and she could furnish fresh meat to the despondent lions and tigers

そして、彼女は落胆したライオンとトラに新鮮な肉を提供することができました

I advised her to keep away from the tree
私は彼女に木に近づかないように忠告しました
She said she wouldn't keep away from the tree
彼女は木から離れないだろうと言った
I foresee trouble and I will emigrate
トラブルを予見して移住します

WEDNESDAY - 水曜日

I have had an eventful time since I escaped
脱出してから波乱に富んだ時間を過ごしました
I escaped on the night she ate from the tree
彼女が木から食べた夜、私は逃げました
and I rode a horse all night as fast as he could go
そして私は彼が行くことができるのと同じくらい速く一晩中馬に乗りました
I hoped to get out of the park and hide in some other country
私は公園から出て、他の国に隠れることを望んでいました
I hoped I would get away before the trouble began
トラブルが始まる前に逃げたいと思っていました
but my plans were not to be
しかし、私の計画はそうではありませんでした
About an hour after sunup I was riding through a flowery plain
日が沈んでから約1時間後、花の咲く平原を走っていました
thousands of animals were grazing and slumbering
何千匹もの動物が放牧され、眠っていました
and the young animals were playing with each other
そして若い動物たちはお互いに遊んでいました
all of a sudden they broke into a tempest of frightful noises
突然、彼らは恐ろしい音の嵐に突入しました
and in one moment the plain was in a frantic commotion
そして一瞬、平原は必死の騒ぎに包まれました
every beast was destroying its neighbour
すべての獣は隣人を破壊していました

I knew what it meant; Eve had eaten that fruit
私はそれが何を意味するのか知っていました。イブはその実を食べていました
death had come into the world
死がこの世にやって来たのです
The tigers ate my horse
トラは私の馬を食べました
they payed no attention when I ordered them to desist
私が彼らにやめるように命じたとき、彼らは注意を払いませんでした
they would even have eaten me if I had stayed
私が残っていたら、彼らは私を食べていただろう
I found this place outside the park
私は公園の外でこの場所を見つけました
I was fairly comfortable for a few days
私は数日間かなり快適でした
but she has found my hiding place
しかし、彼女は私の隠れ場所を見つけました
and she has named the place Tonawanda
そして彼女はその場所をトナワンダと名付けました
she says it looks like Tonawanda
彼女はそれがトナワンダのように見えると言います

In fact, I was not sorry she came
実際、私は彼女が来たことを後悔していませんでした
there are but meagre pickings here
ここにはわずかなピッキングしかありません
and she brought some of those apples
そして彼女はそれらのリンゴのいくつかを持ってきました
I was so hungry that I to eat them
お腹が空いていたので食べたくなりました
eating those apples was against my principles
それらのリンゴを食べることは私の原則に反していました
but I find that principles have no real force except when one is well fed
しかし、私は、原則が十分に供給されているときを除いて、原則は本当の力を持っていないと思います

She came curtained in boughs and bunches of leaves
彼女は枝や葉の束にカーテンで囲まれて来ました
I asked her what she meant by such nonsense
私は彼女にそのようなナンセンスとはどういう意味か尋ねました
I snatched the leaves from her
私は彼女から葉を奪った
and threw her coverings onto the ground
そして彼女の覆いを地面に投げました
she tittered and blushed when I did this
私がこれをしたとき、彼女は震え、顔を赤らめました
I had never seen a person titter and blush before
私はこれまで、人が震えたり赤面したりするのを見たことがありませんでした
her manner seemed to be unbecoming and idiotic
彼女の態度は不愉快でばかげているようでした
but she said I would soon know how it felt
しかし、彼女は私がすぐにそれがどのように感じたかを知るだろうと言いました
in this she was correct
これで彼女は正しかった
I have come to understand the feeling of shame
恥ずかしい気持ちがわかってきました

Hungry as I was, I laid down the apple half eaten
お腹が空いたので、半分食べたリンゴを置きました
it was certainly the best apple I ever saw
それは確かに私が今まで見た中で最高のリンゴでした
it was as especially good apple, considering the lateness of the season
シーズンの遅さを考えると、それは特に良いリンゴでした
and I covered myself in the discarded boughs and branches
そして私は捨てられた枝や枝に身をかがめました
then I spoke to her with some severity
それから私は彼女にいくらかの厳しさで話しました
I ordered her to go and get some more apples
私は彼女に行って、もう少しリンゴを手に入れるように命じ

ました
and I told her not make such a spectacle of herself
そして私は彼女にそのような光景を作らないように言いました
She did as I told her
彼女は私が彼女に言ったようにしました
then we crept down to where the wild beasts bad battled
それから私たちは野獣が悪い戦いをした場所に忍び寄りました
and we collected some of their furs
そして私たちは彼らの毛皮のいくつかを集めました
I made her patch together a couple of suits proper for public occasions
私は彼女に公共の機会にふさわしいいくつかのスーツを一緒にパッチを作りました
They are uncomfortable, it is true
彼らは不快です、それは本当です
but this clothing we now wear is stylish
しかし、私たちが今着ているこの服はスタイリッシュです
and that is the main point about clothes
そしてそれが服についての要点です

I find she is a good companion to have
彼女は良い仲間だと思います
I would be lonesome and depressed without her
彼女がいなければ、私は寂しくて落ち込んでいたでしょう
if I didn't have her I wouldn't have anyone
彼女がいなかったら、誰もいなかったでしょう
but she says it is ordered that we work for our living from now on
しかし、彼女は私たちがこれから私たちの生活のために働くように命じられていると言います
She will be useful in dividing up the work
彼女は仕事を分割するのに役立ちます
I will superintend over the work we do
私は私たちが行う仕事を監督します

Ten Days Later
10日後

She accuses me of being the cause of our disaster!
彼女は私が私たちの災害の原因であると非難します！
She says the Serpent assured her that the forbidden fruit was not apples
彼女は、蛇が禁断の実はリンゴではないことを彼女に保証したと言います
and she says this with apparent sincerity and truth
そして彼女はこれを明らかな誠実さと真実で言います
she says they weren't apples, but instead that they were chestnuts
彼女はそれらがリンゴではなく、代わりに栗だったと言います
I said I was innocent since I had not eaten any chestnuts
私は栗を食べていないので無実だと言いました
but the Serpent informed her that "chestnut" could also have a figurative meaning
しかし、蛇は彼女に「栗」も比喩的な意味を持つことができると知らせました
she says a chestnut can be an aged and mouldy joke
彼女は、栗は古くてカビの生えた冗談になる可能性があると言います
I turned pale at this definition
私はこの定義に青ざめました
because I have made many jokes to pass the weary time
疲れた時間を過ごすためにたくさんの冗談を言ったからです
and some of them my jokes could have been of the chestnut variety
そしてそれらのいくつかは私のジョークが栗の品種であったかもしれません
but I had honestly supposed that they were new jokes when I made them
でも、正直なところ、新しいジョークだと思っていました
She asked me if I had made any jokes just at the time of the catastrophe

彼女は私に、大惨事の時に冗談を言ったかどうか尋ねました
I was obliged to admit that I had made a joke to myself
私は自分自身に冗談を言ったことを認めざるを得ませんでした
although I did not make the joke aloud
私は冗談を声に出してしませんでしたが
this was the joke I was thinking to myself:
これは私が自分自身に考えていた冗談でした:
I was thinking about the waterfalls
滝のことを考えていました
"How wonderful it is to see that vast body of water tumble down there!"
「あの広大な水域が転がり落ちるのを見るのはなんて素晴らしいことでしょう!」
Then in an instant a bright thought flashed into my head
それから一瞬で明るい考えが私の頭に浮かびました
"It would be a great deal more wonderful to see the water tumble up the waterfall!"
「水が滝を転がり落ちるのを見るのはもっと素晴らしいでしょう!」
I was just about to die from laughing when all nature broke loose
すべての自然が解き放たれたとき、私はちょうど笑って死にかけていました
and I had to flee for my life
そして私は私の人生のために逃げなければなりませんでした
"now you see" she said triumphantly
「今、あなたは見る」と彼女は勝ち誇ったように言った
"the Serpent mentioned that very jest"
「蛇はまさにその冗談について言及しました」
"he called it the First Chestnut"
「彼はそれを最初の栗と呼んだ」
"and he said it was coeval with the creation"
「そして彼はそれが創造と同調であると言った」
Alas, I am indeed to blame
悲しいかな、私は確かに責任があります
I wish that I were not so witty

私はそんなに機知に富んでいなかったらいいのにと思います
I wish that I had never had that radiant thought!
あの晴れやかな考えがなかったらよかったのに!

Next Year
来年

We have named it Cain
私たちはそれをカインと名付けました
She caught it while I was up country trapping on the North Shore of the Erie
私がエリーのノースショアで田舎の罠を仕掛けている間に彼女はそれを捕まえました
she caught it in the timber a couple of miles from our dug-out
彼女は私たちの掘り出し物から数マイル離れた材木でそれを捕まえました
or it might have been four miles
または4マイルだったかもしれません
she isn't certain how far it was
彼女はそれがどこまでだったかはわかりません
It resembles us in some ways
それはいくつかの点で私たちに似ています
it may even be a relation to us
それは私たちとの関係でさえあるかもしれません
That is what she thinks
それが彼女の考えです
but this is an error, in my judgement
しかし、私の判断では、これは誤りです
The difference in size suggests it is a new kind of animal
サイズの違いは、それが新しい種類の動物であることを示唆しています
it is perhaps a fish
それはおそらく魚です
though when I put it in the water it sank
私がそれを水に入れると沈んだが

and she plunged in and snatched it out of the water
そして彼女は飛び込んでそれを水から奪いました
so there was no opportunity for the experiment to determine the matter
したがって、実験が問題を決定する機会はありませんでした
I still think it is a fish
私はまだそれが魚だと思う
but she is indifferent about what it is
しかし、彼女はそれが何であるかについて無関心です
and she will not let me have it to try
そして彼女は私にそれを試すことを許しません
I do not understand this
私はこれを理解していません
The coming of the creature seems to have changed her whole nature
生き物の到来は彼女の性質全体を変えたようです
it has made her unreasonable about experiments
それは彼女を実験について不合理にしました
She thinks more of it than she does of any of the other animals
彼女は他のどの動物よりもそれをよく考えています
but she is not able to explain why she likes it so much
しかし、彼女はなぜそれがそんなに好きなのか説明できません
Her mind is disordered
彼女の心は乱れています
everything shows how disordered her mind is
すべてが彼女の心がどれほど乱れているかを示しています
Sometimes she carries the fish in her arms half the night
時々彼女は魚を腕に抱いて夜半を運ぶ
she looks after the fish when it complains
彼女は魚が文句を言うとき、魚の世話をします
I think it complains because it wants to get to the water
水に行きたいから文句を言うと思います
At such times the water comes out of the places that she looks out of
そんな時は、彼女が外に見える場所から水が出てきます

and she pats the fish on the back and makes soft sounds with her mouth
そして彼女は魚の背中を軽くたたき、口で柔らかい音を立てます

she betrays sorrow and solicitude in a hundred ways
彼女は悲しみを裏切り、百の方法で懇願します

I have never seen her do like this with any other fish
私は彼女が他のどの魚でもこのようにするのを見たことがありません

and her actions towards the fish trouble me greatly
そして魚に対する彼女の行動は私を大いに悩ませます

She used to carry the young tigers around like she does with the fish
彼女は魚と同じように若いトラを運び回していました

and she used play with the tigers before we lost our property
そして、彼女は私たちが財産を失う前にタイガースと遊んでいました

but with the tigers she was only playing with them
しかし、タイガースと一緒に彼女は彼らと遊んでいただけでした

she never worried about them when their dinner disagreed with them
彼らの夕食が彼らに同意しなかったとき、彼女は彼らのことを決して心配しませんでした

SUNDAY - 日曜日
She doesn't work Sundays
彼女は日曜日に働きません
but she lies around all tired out
しかし、彼女は疲れ果てて横たわっています
and she likes to have the fish wallow over her
そして彼女は魚を彼女の上にうろつくのが好きです
she makes foolish noises to amuse the fish
彼女は魚を楽しませるために愚かな音を立てます
and she pretends to chew its paws
そして彼女はその足を噛むふりをします
the makes the fish laugh

魚を笑わせる
I have not seen a fish before that could laugh
私は笑うことができる前に魚を見たことがありません
This makes me doubt whether it really is a fish
これは本当に魚であるかどうかを疑わせます
I have come to like Sunday myself
私自身、日曜日が好きになりました
Superintending all the week tires a body so
一週間中監督すると体が疲れるので
There ought to be more Sundays
もっと日曜日があるはずです
In the old days Sundays were tough
昔は日曜日は大変でした
but now Sundays are very handy to have
しかし今、日曜日は持っているととても便利です

WEDNESDAY - 水曜日

It isn't a fish
魚ではありません
I cannot quite make out what it is
私はそれが何であるかを完全に理解することはできません
It makes curious and devilish noises when not satisfied
満足しないと好奇心旺盛で悪魔のような音を立てます
and it says "goo-goo" when it is satisfied
そして、満足すると「グーグー」と書かれています
It is not one of us, for it doesn't walk
それは私たちの一人ではありません、なぜならそれは歩かないからです
it is not a bird, for it doesn't fly
それは飛ばないので、それは鳥ではありません
it is not a frog, for it doesn't hop
それはカエルではありません、なぜならそれは飛び跳ねないからです
it is not a snake, for it doesn't crawl
それは這わないので、それはヘビではありません
I feel sure it is not a fish
魚ではないと確信している

but I cannot get a chance to find out whether it can swim or not
しかし、私はそれが泳ぐことができるかどうかを知る機会を得ることができません
It merely lies around, mostly on its back, with its feet up
それはただ、主に仰向けに、足を上げて横たわっているだけです
I have not seen any other animal do that before
私はこれまで他の動物がそれをするのを見たことがありません
I said I believed it was an enigma
私はそれが謎だと信じていると言いました
but she only admired the word without understanding it
しかし、彼女はそれを理解せずにその言葉を賞賛しただけでした
In my judgement it is either an enigma or some kind of a bug
私の判断では、それは謎かある種のバグのどちらかです
If it dies, I will take it apart and see what its arrangements are
それが死んだら、私はそれを分解して、その配置が何であるかを見ます
I never had a thing perplex me so much
私はこれほど私を困惑させたことはありませんでした

Three Months Later
3ヶ月後

it is only getting more perplexing, instead of less
それは少なくなるのではなく、より当惑しているだけです
I sleep but little
私は寝ますが、少し
it has ceased from lying around
それは横たわっているのをやめました
it goes about on its four legs now
それは今その4本足で歩き回っています

Yet it differs from the other four-legged animals
しかし、それは他の4本足の動物とは異なります
its front legs are unusually short
その前足は異常に短いです
this causes the main part of its body to stick up uncomfortably high
これにより、体の主要部分が不快に高く突き出ます
and this is not attractive
そしてこれは魅力的ではありません
It is built much as we are
それは私たちと同じように構築されています
but its method of travelling shows that it is not of our breed
しかし、その旅行方法は、それが私たちの品種ではないことを示しています
The short front legs and long hind ones indicate that it is of the kangaroo family
短い前足と長い後ろ足は、それがカンガルー科のものであることを示しています
but it is a marked variation of the species
しかし、それは種の著しい変化です
the true kangaroo hops, but this one never does
真のカンガルーホップですが、これは決してしません
Still, it is a curious and interesting variety
それでも、それは好奇心旺盛で興味深い品種です
and it has not been catalogued before
そしてそれは以前にカタログ化されていません
As I discovered it, I feel justified in securing the credit of the discovery
私がそれを発見したとき、私は発見の信用を確保することに正当性があると感じています
and I shall be the one to attach my name to it
そして私はそれに私の名前を付ける人になるでしょう
so I have called it Kangaroorum Adamiensis
だから私はそれをカンガルーラムアダミエンシスと呼んでいます

It must have been a young one when it came
それが来たとき、それは若いものだったに違いありません
because it has grown exceedingly since it came
それが来てから非常に成長したからです
It must be five times as big, now, as it was then
今は当時の5倍の大きさになっているに違いありません
when discontented it can make twenty-two to thirty-eight times the noise it made at first
不満があると、最初に作った音の22倍から38倍の音を立てることができます
Coercion does not modify this
強制はこれを変更しません
if anything, coercion has the contrary effect
どちらかといえば、強制には逆の効果があります
For this reason I discontinued the system
このため、私はシステムを中止しました
She reconciles it by persuasion
彼女は説得によってそれを和解させます
and she gives it things which she had previously told it she wouldn't give it
そして、彼女は以前にそれを与えないと言ったものをそれに与えます
As already observed, I was not at home when it first came
すでに観察したように、それが最初に来たとき、私は家にいませんでした
and she told me she found it in the woods
そして彼女は森の中でそれを見つけたと私に言いました
It seems odd that it should be the only one
それだけであるべきだというのは奇妙に思えます
yet it must be the only one
しかし、それだけに違いありません
I have worn myself out trying to find another one
私は別のものを見つけようとして疲れ果てています
if I had another one in my collection I could study it better
私のコレクションに別のものがあれば、もっとよく勉強することができます
and then this one would have one of its kind to play with

そして、これはその種の1つで遊ぶでしょう
surely, then it would be quieter
確かに、それならそれは静かになるでしょう
and then we could tame it more easily
そして、私たちはそれをより簡単に飼いならすことができました
But I find none, nor any vestige of any
しかし、私には何も見当たらず、その痕跡も見つかりません
and strangest of all, I have found no tracks
そして何よりも奇妙なことに、私はトラックを見つけていません
It has to live on the ground
それは地上に住んでいなければなりません
it cannot help itself
それはそれ自体を助けることはできません
therefore, how does it get about without leaving a track?
したがって、トラックを離れることなくどのように移動しますか？
I have set a dozen traps
私はダースの罠を仕掛けました
but the traps do no good
しかし、罠は役に立たない
I catch all the small animals except that one
あれ以外の小動物を全部捕まえる
animals that merely go into the trap out of curiosity
好奇心から罠にかかっただけの動物
I think they go to see what the milk is there for
彼らはミルクが何のためにあるのかを見に行くと思います
but they never drink this milk
しかし、彼らはこのミルクを決して飲みません

Three Months Later
3ヶ月後

The kangaroo still continues to grow
カンガルーはまだ成長を続けています
this continual growth is very strange and perplexing
この継続的な成長は非常に奇妙で当惑しています
I never knew any animal to spend so much time growing
こんなに多くの時間を費やす動物を知りませんでした
It has fur on its head now, but not like kangaroo fur
今は頭に毛皮がありますが、カンガルーの毛皮のようではありません
it's exactly like our hair, but finer and softer
それは私たちの髪とまったく同じですが、より細かくて柔らかいです
and instead of being black its fur is red
そして、その毛皮は黒ではなく赤です
I am like to lose my mind over this zoological freak
私はこの動物学のフリークに気を失うようなものです
the capricious and harassing developments are unclassifiable
気まぐれで嫌がらせの展開は分類できません
If only I could catch another one
もう一匹釣れたらいいのに
but it is hopeless trying to find another
しかし、別のものを見つけようとするのは絶望的です
I have to accept that it is a new variety
私はそれが新しい品種であることを受け入れなければなりません
it is the only sample, this is plain to see
それは唯一のサンプルです、これは見るのが明白です
But I caught a true kangaroo and brought it in
でも本物のカンガルーを捕まえて持ち込んだ
I thought that this one might be lonesome
これは寂しいかもしれないと思いました
so it might prefer to have a kangaroo for company
だから、会社のためにカンガルーを持っていることを好むか

もしれません
otherwise it would have no kin at all
そうでなければ、それはまったく親族を持たないでしょう
and it would have no animal that it could feel a nearness to
そして、それはそれが近さを感じることができる動物を持っていないでしょう
this way it might get sympathy for its forlorn condition among strangers
このようにして、見知らぬ人の間でその決死隊の状態に同情するかもしれません
strangers who do not know its ways or habits
その方法や習慣を知らない見知らぬ人
strangers who do not know how to make it feel that it is among friends
それが友人の間にあると感じさせる方法を知らない見知らぬ人
but it was a mistake
しかし、それは間違いでした
it went into terrible fits at the sight of the kangaroo
それはカンガルーを見てひどいフィット感になりました
I am convinced it had never seen a kangaroo before
カンガルーを見たことがないと確信しています
I pity the poor noisy little animal
かわいそうな騒々しい小動物を哀れに思います
but there is nothing I can do to make it happy
しかし、それを幸せにするために私にできることは何もありません
I would like to tame it, but that is out of the question
飼いならしたいのですが、それは問題外です
the more I try, the worse I seem to make it
努力すればするほど、私はそれを悪化させるようです
It grieves me to the heart to see it in its little storms of sorrow and passion
悲しみと情熱の小さな嵐の中でそれを見るのは私を心に悲しませます
I wanted to let it go, but she wouldn't hear of it
私はそれを手放したかったのですが、彼女はそれを聞いてい

ませんでした
That seemed cruel and not like her
それは残酷で彼女のようではないようでした
and yet she may be right
それでも彼女は正しいかもしれません
It might be lonelier than ever
今まで以上に寂しいかもしれません
if I cannot find another one, how could it not be lonely?
別のものが見つからないのなら、どうして寂しくないのでしょうか。

Five Months Later
5ヶ月後

It is not a kangaroo
カンガルーではありません
holding her fingers it goes a few steps on its hind legs
彼女の指を持って、それはその後ろ足で数歩進みます
and then it falls down again
そして、それは再び落ちます
so it is probably some kind of a bear
だからそれはおそらくある種のクマです
and yet it has no tail, as yet
それでも、まだ尻尾がありません
and it has no fur, except on its head
そしてそれは頭を除いて毛皮を持っていません
It still keeps on growing, which is very interesting
それはまだ成長し続けており、それは非常に興味深いものです
bears get their growth earlier than this
クマはこれより早く成長します
Bears are dangerous since our catastrophe
私たちの大惨事以来、クマは危険です
soon it will have to have a muzzle on
すぐにそれは銃口をつけなければならないでしょう
otherwise I won't feel safe around it

そうでなければ、私はそれの周りで安全だとは感じません
I have offered to get her a kangaroo if she would let this one go
彼女がこれを手放すなら、私は彼女にカンガルーを手に入れることを申し出ました
but she did not appreciate my offer
しかし、彼女は私の申し出に感謝しませんでした
she is determined to run us into all sorts of foolish risks
彼女は私たちをあらゆる種類の愚かなリスクに追いやろうと決心しています
she was not like this before she lost her mind
彼女は気を失う前はこんな感じではなかった

A Fortnight Later
2週間後

I examined its mouth
私はその口を調べました
There is no danger yet; it has only one tooth
まだ危険はありません。歯は1本しかありません
It has no tail yet
まだ尻尾がありません
It makes more noise now than it ever did before
それは今、これまで以上に多くの音を立てます
and it makes the noise mainly at night
そしてそれは主に夜に音を立てます
I have moved out
引っ越しました
But I shall go over in the mornings to breakfast
しかし、私は朝に朝食に行きます
then I will see if it has more teeth
それから私はそれがより多くの歯を持っているかどうかを確認します
If it gets a mouthful of teeth, it will be time for it to go
それが一口の歯を得るならば、それはそれが行く時間になるでしょう

I won't make an exception if it has no tail
尻尾がない場合は例外を作りません
bears do not need tails in order to be dangerous
クマは危険であるために尾を必要としません

Four Months Later
4ヶ月後

I have been off hunting and fishing a month
私は一ヶ月狩猟と釣りを休んでいます
up in the region that she calls Buffalo
彼女がバッファローと呼ぶ地域で
I don't know why she has called it Buffalo
なぜ彼女がそれをバッファローと呼んだのかわかりません
it could be because there are not any buffaloes there
そこに水牛がいないからかもしれません
the bear has learned to paddle around all by itself
クマは自分でパドルすることを学びました
it can walk on its hind legs
後ろ足で歩くことができます
and it says "daddy" and "mummy" to us
そしてそれは私たちに「パパ」と「ミイラ」と言います
It is certainly a new species
それは確かに新種です
This resemblance to words may be purely accidental, of course
もちろん、この言葉との類似性は、まったくの偶然かもしれません
it may be that its words have no purpose or meaning
その言葉には目的や意味がないのかもしれません
but even in that case it would still be extraordinary
しかし、その場合でも、それはまだ並外れたことです
using words is something which no other bear can do
言葉を使うことは、他のクマにはできないことです
This imitation of speech sufficiently indicates that this is a new kind of bear

このスピーチの模倣は、これが新しい種類のクマであること
を十分に示しています
add to that the general absence of fur
それに加えて、毛皮の一般的な欠如
and consider the entire absence of a tail
そして尾の完全な不在を考慮してください
further study of it will be exceedingly interesting
それのさらなる研究は非常に興味深いでしょう
Meantime I will go off on a far expedition among the forests of the North
その間、私は北の森の中を遠く離れた遠征に出かけます
there I will make a more exhaustive search
そこで私はより徹底的な検索をします
There must certainly be another one somewhere
確かにどこかに別のものがあるに違いありません
this one will be less dangerous when it has company of its own species
これは、独自の種の会社がある場合、危険性が低くなります
I will go straightway
まっすぐ進みます
but I will muzzle this one first
しかし、私は最初にこれを口輪にします

Three Months Later
3ヶ月後

It has been a weary, weary hunt
それは疲れた、疲れた狩りでした
yet I have had no success
しかし、私は成功していません
while I was gone she caught another one!
私がいなくなっている間に、彼女は別のものを捕まえました!
and she didn't even leave the estate
そして彼女は地所を離れさえしませんでした
I never saw such luck
私はそのような運を見たことがありません

I might have hunted these woods a hundred years without finding one
私はこれらの森を100年も見つからずに狩ったかもしれません

Next Day - 翌日
I have been comparing the new one with the old one
私は新しいものと古いものを比較しています
it is perfectly plain that they are the same breed
それらが同じ品種であることは完全に明白です
I was going to stuff one of them for my collection
私は私のコレクションのためにそれらの1つを詰めるつもりでした
but she is prejudiced against it for some reason
しかし、彼女は何らかの理由でそれに対して偏見を持っています
so I have relinquished the idea
だから私はその考えを放棄しました
but I think it is a mistake
しかし、それは間違いだと思います
It would be an irreparable loss to science if they should get away
彼らが逃げるべきなら、それは科学にとって取り返しのつかない損失になるでしょう
The old one is tamer than it was
古いものは以前よりも飼いならされています
now it can laugh and talk like the parrot
今、それはオウムのように笑って話すことができます
I have no doubt that it has learned this from the parrot
私はそれがオウムからこれを学んだことは間違いありません
I calculate it has a great amount of the imitative faculty
私はそれが模倣的な能力を大量に持っていると計算します
I shall be astonished if it turns out to be a new kind of parrot
それが新しい種類のオウムであることが判明した場合、私は驚くでしょう
and yet I ought not to be astonished
それでも私は驚くべきではありません
because it has already been everything else it could think of

それはすでにそれが考えることができる他のすべてだったからです
The new one is as ugly now as the old one was at first
新しいものは、古いものが最初だったのと同じくらい醜いです
it has the same sulphur complexion
それは同じ硫黄の顔色をしています
and it has the same singular head without any fur on it
そしてそれはそれに毛皮のない同じ特異な頭を持っています
She calls the new one Abel
彼女は新しいものをアベルと呼んでいます

Ten Years Later
それから10年後

They are boys; we found it out long ago
彼らは男の子です。私たちはずっと前にそれを見つけました
It was their coming in that small, immature shape that puzzled us
私たちを困惑させたのは、その小さくて未熟な形で彼らが来たことでした
we were not used to animals being so small for so long
私たちは長い間、動物がそれほど小さいことに慣れていませんでした
There are some girls now
今は女の子がいます
Abel is a good boy
アベルはいい子です
but if Cain had stayed a bear it would have improved him
しかし、カインがクマのままだったら、それは彼を改善したでしょう

After all these years I realize I had made a mistake
何年も経った後、私は間違いを犯したことに気づきました
I see that I was initially mistaken about Eve
最初はイブについて間違っていたようです
it is better to live outside the Garden with her than inside it without her
彼女なしで庭の中に住むよりも、彼女と一緒に庭の外に住む方が良いです
At first I thought she talked too much
最初は彼女が話しすぎだと思いました
but now I should be sorry to have that voice fall silent
しかし今、私はその声が沈黙するのを残念に思うべきです

I wouldn't want that voice to pass out of my life
その声が私の人生から消えてほしくない
Blessed be the chestnut that brought us together
私たちを結びつけた栗に祝福あれ
this chestnut has taught me to know the goodness of her heart
この栗は私に彼女の心の良さを知ることを教えてくれました
this chestnut has taught me the sweetness of her spirit!
この栗は私に彼女の精神の甘さを教えてくれました!

- Eve's Diary-
-イブの日記-
Translated from the original, by Mark Twain
原文からの翻訳、マーク・トウェイン

SATURDAY - 土曜日
I am almost a whole day old, now
私は今、ほぼ丸一日です
I arrived yesterday
昨日到着しました
That is as it seems to me
それは私には思えます
And it must be so
そしてそれはそうに違いありません
perhaps there was a day-before-yesterday

もしかしたら一昨日のことがあったのかもしれない
but I was not there when it happened
しかし、それが起こったとき、私はそこにいませんでした
if I had been there I would remember it
もし私がそこにいたら、私はそれを覚えていたでしょう
It could be, of course, that it did happen
もちろん、それが起こった可能性があります
and it could be that I was not noticing
そして、それは私が気づいていなかったのかもしれません
Very well; I will be very watchful now
非常にいいです；これからは気をつけます
if a day-before-yesterday happen I will make a note
一昨日の出来事が起こったら、私はメモを取ります
It will be best to start right
正しく始めるのが最善です
and it's best not to let the record get confused
そして、レコードを混乱させないことが最善です
I feel these details are going to be important
これらの詳細が重要になると思います
my instincts are telling me this
私の本能は私にこれを教えてくれます
they might be important to historians some day
それらはいつか歴史家にとって重要かもしれません
For I feel like an experiment
私は実験のように感じるからです
I feel exactly like an experiment
まるで実験のようです
a person can't feel more like an experiment than I do
人は私よりも実験のように感じることはできません
it would be impossible to feel more like an experiment
実験のように感じることは不可能でしょう
and so I am coming to feel convinced that is what I am
そして、それが私であると確信するようになっています
I am an experiment
私は実験です
just an experiment and nothing more
単なる実験であり、それ以上のものはありません

Then, if I am an experiment, am I the whole of it?
では、もし私が実験だとしたら、その全部なのだろうか。
No, I think I am not the whole experiment
いいえ、私は実験全体ではないと思います
I think the rest of it is part of the experiment too
それの残りの部分も実験の一部だと思います
I am the main part of the experiment
私は実験の主要部分です
but I think the rest of it has its share in the matter
しかし、私はそれの残りの部分が問題にそのシェアを持っているると思います
Is my position in the experiment assured?
実験における私の立場は保証されていますか?
or do I have to watch my position and take care of it?

それとも私は自分の立場を見てそれを世話する必要がありますか?
I think it is the latter, perhaps
おそらく後者だと思います
Some instinct tells me guard my role
いくつかの本能は私に私の役割を守ることを教えてくれます
eternal vigilance is the price of supremacy
永遠の警戒は覇権の代償です
That is a good phrase, I think
それは良いフレーズだと思います
it is especially good for someone so young
それはとても若い人にとって特に良いです

- 41 -

Everything looks better today than it did yesterday
昨日よりも今日はすべてが良く見えます
there had been a great rush of finishing up the mountains
山を仕上げるという大きなラッシュがありました
so things had been left in a ragged condition
そのため、物事はぼろぼろの状態のままでした
and the open plains were so cluttered that
そして、開いた平原はとても雑然としていたので、
all the aspects and proportions were quite distressing
すべての側面とプロポーションは非常に苦痛でした
because they still had rubbish and remnants
彼らはまだゴミや残骸を持っていたので
Noble and beautiful works of art should not be rushed
高貴で美しい芸術作品は急いではいけません
and this majestic new world is indeed a work of art
そして、この壮大な新しい世界は確かに芸術作品です
I can tell it has been made to be noble and beautiful
高貴で美しいように作られていることがわかります
and it is certainly marvellously near to being perfect
そして、それは確かに完璧に近づいています
notwithstanding the shortness of the time
時間の短さにもかかわらず
There are too many stars in some places
場所によっては星が多すぎます
and there are not enough stars in other places
そして他の場所には十分な星がありません
but that can be remedied soon enough, no doubt
しかし、それは間違いなくすぐに修正することができます
The moon got loose last night and slid down
昨夜は月がゆるんで滑り落ちました
it fell out of the scheme
それは計画から外れました
this was a very great loss
これは非常に大きな損失でした
it breaks my heart to think of it
それを考えると心が痛む
among the ornaments and decorations it is unique

装飾品や装飾品の中でそれはユニークです
nothing is comparable to it for beauty and finish
美しさと仕上がりに匹敵するものはありません
It should have been held in place better
それはよりよく所定の位置に保持されるべきでした
I wish we could get it back again
また取り戻せたらいいのにと思います

But there is no telling where it went to
しかし、それがどこに行ったのかはわかりません
And besides, whoever gets it will hide it
その上、それを手に入れた人は誰でもそれを隠します
I know it because I would do it myself
自分でやるので知っています

I believe I can be honest in all other matters
私は他のすべての問題に正直になることができると信じています
but I already begin to realize something;
しかし、私はすでに何かに気づき始めています。
the core of my nature is love of the beautiful
私の性質の核心は美しいものへの愛です
I have a passion for the beautiful
私は美しいものに情熱を持っています
so it would not be safe to trust me with a moon
ですから、私を月に信頼するのは安全ではありません
I could give up a moon that I found in the daytime
昼間に見つけた月をあきらめることができました
because I would be afraid someone was looking
誰かが見ているのではないかと心配するからです
but if I found a moon in the dark I would keep it
しかし、暗闇の中で月を見つけたら、それを維持します
I am sure I could find some kind of an excuse
私はある種の言い訳を見つけることができると確信しています
I would find a way to not say anything about it
私はそれについて何も言わない方法を見つけるでしょう
because I do love moons
私は月が大好きだからです
they are so pretty and so romantic
彼らはとてもきれいでとてもロマンチックです
I wish we had five or six of them
5つか6つあったらいいのにと思います
I would never go to bed
私は決して寝ません
I would never get tired lying on the moss-bank
苔の土手に横たわっていても飽きません
and I would always be looking up at them
そして私はいつも彼らを見上げていました

Stars are good, too
星も良いです
I wish I could get some to put in my hair
髪に入れるものがあればいいのにと思います
But I suppose I can never do that
しかし、私はそれを決してできないと思います
it's surprising how far away they are
彼らがどれほど離れているかは驚くべきことです
because they do not look like they're far away
彼らは遠くにいるようには見えないからです
they first showed themselves last night
彼らは昨夜最初に現れました
I tried to knock some down with a pole

ポールでいくつかを倒してみました
but it didn't reach, which astonished me;
しかし、それは届かなかったので、私は驚きました。
then I tried throwing clods at them
それから私は彼らに土塊を投げてみました
I tried this till I was all tired out
私はすべて疲れるまでこれを試しました
but I never managed to get one
しかし、私はそれを手に入れることができませんでした
It must be because I am left-handed
それは私が左利きだからに違いありません
because of this I cannot throw good
このため、私は良いものを投げることができません
though I did make some close shots
私はいくつかのクローズショットをしましたが
I saw the black blot of the clod
塊の黒いしみが見えました
it sailed right into the midst of the golden clusters
それは黄金のクラスターの真っ只中に航海しました
I must have tried forty or fifty times
私は40回か50回試したに違いありません
and I just barely missed them
そして私はそれらをかろうじて逃しました
perhaps I should have held out a little longer
もう少し我慢すべきだったのかもしれません
and then I might have got one
そして、私はそれを持っているかもしれません

So I cried a little, which was natural
だから私は少し泣きました、それは自然なことでした
I suppose it is natural for one of my age
私の年齢の1人にとっては当然のことだと思います
and after I was rested I got a basket
そして私が休んだ後、私はバスケットを手に入れました
I went to a hill on the extreme rim of the circle
円の一番端にある丘に行ってきました
there the stars should be closer to the ground
そこで星は地面に近いはずです
perhaps if I was there I could get them
おそらく私がそこにいたら、私はそれらを手に入れることができました
then I could get them with my hands

それから私は私の手でそれらを手に入れることができました
this would be better anyway
とにかくこれは良いでしょう
because then I could gather them tenderly
そうすれば、私はそれらを優しく集めることができたからです
and I would not break them
そして私はそれらを壊しません
But it was farther than I thought
しかし、思ったより遠かった
and at last I had to give it up
そしてついに私はそれをあきらめなければなりませんでした
I was so tired from all my trying
私はすべての努力からとても疲れていました
I couldn't drag my feet another step
もう一歩足を引きずることができませんでした
and besides, my feet were sore
その上、私の足は痛かった
and my feet hurt me very much
そして私の足は私をとても傷つけました
I couldn't get back home
家に帰れなかった
it was late, and turning cold
遅くなり、寒くなりました
but I found some tigers
しかし、私はいくつかのトラを見つけました
and I nestled in among them
そして私は彼らの中に寄り添いました
and it was most adorably comfortable
そして、それは最も愛らしいほど快適でした
and their breath was sweet and pleasant
そして彼らの息は甘くて心地よかった
because they live on a diet of strawberries
彼らはイチゴの食事で暮らしているからです
I had never seen a tiger before
私はこれまで虎を見たことがありませんでした
but I knew straight away by their stripes

しかし、私は彼らの縞模様ですぐにわかりました
If only I could have one of those skins
私がそれらのスキンの1つを持つことができれば
it would make a lovely gown
それは素敵なガウンを作るでしょう

Today I am getting better ideas about distances
今日、私は距離についてより良いアイデアを得ています
I was so eager to get hold of every pretty thing
私はすべてのきれいなものを手に入れたいととても熱望していました
I was so eager that I giddily grabbed for it
私はとても熱心だったので、ぼんやりとそれをつかみました

sometimes I grabbed for it when it was too far away
遠すぎるときにつかむこともありました
and I grabbed for it when it was but six inches away
そして私はそれがわずか6インチ離れたときにそれをつかみました
I even grabbed for it when it was between thorns!
それがとげの間にあるとき、私はそれをつかみました!
I learned a lesson and I made an axiom
私は教訓を学び、公理を作りました
I made it all out of my own head
私は自分の頭からそれをすべて作りました
it is my very first one
それは私の最初のものです
THE SCRATCHED EXPERIMENT SHUNS THE THORN
引っかき傷のある実験はとげを避けます
I think it is a very good axiom for one so young
とても若い人にとっては非常に良い公理だと思います

last afternoon I followed the other experiment around
最後の午後、私は他の実験を追いかけました
I kept a distance, to see what it might be for
私はそれが何のためにあるのかを見るために距離を保ちました
But I was not able to establish its use
しかし、私はその使用を確立することができませんでした
I think it is a man
男だと思います
I had never seen a man
私は男を見たことがありませんでした
but it looked like a man
しかし、それは男のように見えました
and I feel sure that that is what it is
そして私はそれがそれが何であるかを確信しています
I realized something strange about this man
私はこの男について奇妙なことに気づきました
I feel more curiosity about it than the other reptiles
他の爬虫類よりも好奇心を感じます

I'm assuming it is a reptile
私はそれが爬虫類であると仮定しています
because it has frowzy hair and blue eyes
それは眉をひそめた髪と青い目をしているからです
and it looks like a reptile
そしてそれは爬虫類のように見えます
It has no hips and tapers like a carrot when it stands
腰がなく、立っているとニンジンのように先細になっています

it spreads itself apart like a derrick
それはデリックのようにバラバラに広がります
so I think it is a reptile
だから私はそれが爬虫類だと思います
although it may be architecture
それは建築かもしれませんが
I was afraid of it at first
最初は怖かったです
and I started to run every time it turned around
そして、それが向きを変えるたびに走り始めました
because I thought it was going to chase me
追いかけてくると思ったから
but by and by I found it was only trying to get away
しかし、やがて私はそれが逃げようとしているだけであることに気づきました
so after that I was not timid any more
その後、私はもう臆病ではありませんでした
but I tracked behind it by about twenty yards
しかし、私はそれの後ろを約20ヤード追跡しました
I tracked it for several hours
私はそれを数時間追跡しました
this made it nervous and unhappy
これはそれを緊張させ、不幸にしました
At last it was a good deal worried, and climbed a tree
とうとうかなり心配して、木に登りました
I waited a good while
私はしばらく待った
then I gave it up and went home
それからそれをあきらめて家に帰りました

SUNDAY - 日曜日
Today the same thing happened
今日も同じことが起こりました
I got it up the tree again
私は再びそれを木に登りました
It is still up there
それはまだそこにあります
and it is resting, apparently
そしてそれはどうやら休んでいます
But that is a subterfuge
しかし、それは卑劣です
Sunday isn't the day of rest
日曜日は休息の日ではありません
Saturday is appointed for that

そのために土曜日が指定されています
It looks to me like a strange creature
それは私には奇妙な生き物のように見えます
it is more interested in resting than in anything else
それは何よりも休むことに興味があります
It would tire me to rest so much
そんなに休むのは疲れます
It tires me just to sit around and watch the tree
座って木を見るだけで疲れます
I do wonder what it is for
私はそれが何のためなのか疑問に思います
I never see it do anything
私はそれが何もするのを見ません

They returned the moon last night
彼らは昨夜月を返しました
and I was SO happy!
そして私はとても幸せでした!
I think it is very honest of them
とても正直だと思います
It slid down and fell off again
それは滑り落ちて再び落ちました
but I was not distressed
しかし、私は苦しんでいませんでした
there is no need to worry
心配する必要はありません
when one has such kind neighbours, they will fetch it back
そのような親切な隣人がいるとき、彼らはそれを取り戻すでしょう
I wish I could do something to show my appreciation
感謝の気持ちを伝えるために何かできたらいいのにと思います
I would like to send them some stars
私は彼らにいくつかの星を送りたいです
because we have more than we can use
使える以上のものがあるからです
I do mean to say I, not we
私は私たちではなく私と言うつもりです
I can see that the reptile cares nothing for such things
爬虫類はそのようなことを何も気にしないことがわかります
It has low tastes and it is not kind
味が少なくて優しくない
I went there yesterday evening
昨日の夕方に行きました
in the evening it had crept down
夕方には忍び寄っていた
and it was trying to catch the little speckled fishes
そして、それは小さな斑点のある魚を捕まえようとしていました
the little fishes that play in the pool
プールで遊ぶ小さな魚

and I had to clod it
そして私はそれを土塊にしなければなりませんでした
in order to make it go up the tree again
それを再び木に登らせるために
and then it left them alone
そして、それは彼らを放っておいた
I wonder if that is what it is for?
それが何のためなのかしら？
Hasn't it any heart?
心はありませんか？
Hasn't it any compassion for the little creature?
それは小さな生き物への思いやりではありませんか？
was it designed and manufactured for such ungentle work?
それはそのような不親切な仕事のために設計され、製造されましたか？
It has the look of being made for silly things
それはばかげたもののために作られているように見えます
One of the clods hit the back of its ear
塊の1つが耳の後ろに当たった
and it used language, which gave me a thrill
そして、それは私にスリルを与えた言語を使用しました
for it was the first time I had ever heard speech
スピーチを聞いたのは初めてだったからです
it was the first speech I heard except my own
それは私が自分のスピーチを除いて聞いた最初のスピーチでした
I did not understand the words
言葉がわからなかった
but the words seemed expressive
しかし、その言葉は表現力豊かに見えました

When I found it could talk I felt a new interest in it
それが話すことができるとわかったとき、私はそれに新たな興味を感じました
because I love to talk more than anything
私は何よりも話すのが好きだからです
I like to talk all day
私は一日中話すのが好きです
and in my sleep I talk too
そして私の睡眠中に私も話します
and I am very interesting
そして私はとても面白いです

but if I had another to talk to I could be twice as interesting
しかし、私が話す別の人がいたら、私は2倍面白いかもしれません
and I would never stop talking
そして私は話すのをやめません

If this reptile is a man, it isn't an it, is it?
この爬虫類が人間なら、それはそれではありませんね。
That wouldn't be grammatical, would it?
それは文法的ではないでしょう?
I think it would be he
それは彼だろうと思います
In that case one would parse it thus:
その場合、次のように解析します。

nominative; he
主格;彼
dative; him
与格;彼
possessive; his
所有;彼の
Well, I will consider it a man
まあ、私はそれを男と見なします
and I will call it he until it turns out to be something else
そしてそれが何か他のものであることが判明するまで私はそれを彼と呼びます
This will be handier than having so many uncertainties
これは、非常に多くの不確実性を持つよりも便利です

NEXT WEEK SUNDAY
来週の日曜日
All the week I tagged around after him
一週間中、私は彼の後にタグを付けました
and I tried to get acquainted with him
そして私は彼と知り合いになろうとしました
I had to do the talking because he was shy
彼は恥ずかしがり屋だったので、私は話をしなければなりませんでした
but I didn't mind talking
しかし、私は話すことを気にしませんでした
He seemed pleased to have me around
彼は私と一緒にいることを喜んでいるようでした
and I used the sociable 'we' a good deal
そして私は社交的な「私たち」をかなり使いました
because it seemed to flatter him to be included
彼が含まれていることをお世辞にしているように見えたからです

WEDNESDAY - 水曜日

We are getting along very well now
私たちは今とても仲良くしています
and we're getting better and better acquainted
そして、私たちはどんどんよくなっています
He does not try to avoid me any more, which is a good sign
彼はもう私を避けようとはしません、それは良い兆候です
and it shows that he likes to have me with him, which pleases me
そしてそれは彼が私を彼と一緒にいるのが好きであることを示しています、それは私を喜ばせます
and I study to be useful to him
そして私は彼に役立つように勉強します
I want to be useful in every way I can
あらゆる面で役に立ちたい
so as to increase his regard of me
彼の私への敬意を高めるために

During the last day or two
最後の一日か二日の間に
I have taken all the work of naming things off his hands
私は彼の手から物事に名前を付けるすべての仕事を取り除いた
and this has been a great relief to him
そして、これは彼にとって大きな安堵でした
for he has no gift in that line of work
彼はその仕事のラインに贈り物を持っていないからです
and he is evidently very grateful
そして彼は明らかにとても感謝しています
He can't think of a rational name to save himself
彼は自分自身を救うための合理的な名前を考えることができません

but I do not let him see that I am aware of his defect
しかし、私は彼に私が彼の欠陥を知っていることを見させません

Whenever a new creature comes along I name it
新しい生き物がやってくるたびに、私はそれに名前を付けます

before he has time to expose himself by an awkward silence
彼が気まずい沈黙によって自分自身をさらす時間がある前に

In this way I have saved him many embarrassments
このようにして、私は彼に多くの恥ずかしさを救ってきました

I have no defect like this
このような欠陥はありません

The minute I set eyes on an animal I know what it is
動物に目を向けた瞬間、それが何であるかがわかります

I don't have to reflect even for a moment
一瞬たりとも反省しなくていい

the right name comes out instantly
正しい名前がすぐに出てきます

just as if it were an inspiration
まるでインスピレーションであるかのように

I have no doubt it is
私はそれが間違いありません

because I am sure it wasn't in me half a minute before
30分前には私の中になかったと確信しているからです

I seem to know just by the shape of the creature
生き物の形だけでわかるようです

and I know from the way it acts what animal it is
そして私はそれがどんな動物であるかを行動する方法から知っています

When the dodo came along he thought it was a wildcat
ドードーがやってきたとき、彼はそれが山猫だと思った
I saw it in his eyes
私は彼の目にそれを見ました
But I saved him from embarrassment
しかし、私は彼を恥ずかしさから救いました
I was careful not to do it in a way that could hurt his pride
彼のプライドを傷つけるようなことをしないように気をつけました
I just spoke up as if pleasantly surprised
私は嬉しそうに驚いたように声を上げた
I didn't speak as if I was dreaming of conveying information
情報を伝えることを夢見ているかのように話しませんでした
"Well, I do declare, if there isn't the dodo!"

「まあ、ドードーがなければ宣言します!」
I explained without seeming to be explaining
私は説明しているようには見えずを説明しました
I explained how I knew it was a dodo
私はそれがドードーだと知った方法を説明しました
I thought maybe he was a little piqued
多分彼は少し腹を立てていると思いました
I knew the creature when he didn't
彼が知らなかったとき、私はその生き物を知っていました
but it was quite evident that he admired me
しかし、彼が私を賞賛していることは非常に明白でした
That was very agreeable
それは非常に賛成でした
and I thought of it more than once with gratification before I slept
そして私は眠る前に満足してそれを何度も考えました
How little a thing can make us happy
どんな小さなことでも幸せになれる
we're happy when we feel that we have earned it!
獲得したと感じたときは嬉しいです!

THURSDAY - 木曜日
my first sorrow
私の最初の悲しみ
Yesterday he avoided me
昨日彼は私を避けました
and he seemed to wish I would not talk to him
そして彼は私が彼と話さないことを望んでいるようでした
I could not believe it
信じられませんでした
and I thought there was some mistake
そして私はいくつかの間違いがあると思った
because I loved to be with him
私は彼と一緒にいるのが大好きだったので
and loved to hear him talk
そして彼が話すのを聞くのが大好きでした
and so how could it be that he could feel unkind toward me?
それで、どうして彼は私に対して不親切に感じることができたのでしょうか?
I had not done anything wrong
私は何も悪いことをしていませんでした
But it seemed true, so I went away
しかし、それは本当だったので、私は去りました
and I sat lonely in the place where I first saw him
そして私は最初に彼に会った場所に孤独に座っていました
on the morning that we were made
私たちが作られた朝に
when I did not know what he was
私が彼が何であるかを知らなかったとき
when I was still indifferent about him
私がまだ彼に無関心だったとき
but now it was a mournful place
しかし今、それは悲惨な場所でした
and every little thing spoke of him
そして、すべての小さなことが彼について話しました
and my heart was very sore
そして私の心はとても痛かった
I did not really know why I was feeling like this

なぜこんな気持ちになっているのかよくわかりませんでした
because it was a new feeling
新しい感覚だったので
I had not experienced it before
私は以前にそれを経験したことがありませんでした
and it was all a mystery to me
そしてそれは私にとってすべて謎でした
and I could not make sense of it
そして私はそれを理解することができませんでした

But when night came I could not bear the lonesomeness
しかし、夜になると寂しさに耐えられなくなりました
I went to the new shelter which he had built
私は彼が建てた新しい避難所に行きました

I went to ask him what I had done that was wrong
私は彼に私が何をしたのか尋ねに行きました
and I wanted to know how I could mend it
そして私はそれをどのように修復できるか知りたかったのです
I wanted to get back his kindness again
もう一度彼の優しさを取り戻したかった
but he put me out in the rain
しかし、彼は私を雨の中に出しました
and it was my first sorrow
そしてそれは私の最初の悲しみでした

SUNDAY - 日曜日

It is pleasant again and now I am happy
それは再び楽しいです、そして今私は幸せです
but those were heavy days
しかし、それらは重い日でした
I do not think of those days when I can help it
私はそれを助けることができるそれらの日を考えていません

I tried to get him some of those apples
私は彼にそれらのリンゴのいくつかを手に入れようとしました
but I cannot learn to throw straight
しかし、私はまっすぐに投げることを学ぶことができません
I failed, but I think the good intention pleased him
私は失敗しましたが、善意が彼を喜ばせたと思います
They are forbidden
彼らは禁じられています
and he says I would come to harm if I ate one
そして彼は私がそれを食べたら私が害を及ぼすだろうと言います
but then I would come to harm through pleasing him
しかし、それから私は彼を喜ばせることによって害を及ぼすようになるでしょう
why should I care for that harm?
なぜ私はその害を気にする必要がありますか?

MONDAY
月曜日

This morning I told him my name
今朝、私は彼に私の名前を話しました
I hoped it would interest him
私はそれが彼の興味を引くことを望みました
But he did not care for it, which is strange
しかし、彼はそれを気にしませんでした、それは奇妙です
If he should tell me his name I would care
彼が私に彼の名前を教えてくれるなら、私は気にするでしょう
I think it would be pleasanter in my ears than any other sound
他のどの音よりも耳に心地よいと思います

He talks very little
彼はほとんど話しません
Perhaps it is because he is not bright
おそらくそれは彼が明るくないからです
and maybe he is sensitive about his intellect
そして多分彼は彼の知性に敏感です
it could be that he wishes to conceal it
彼はそれを隠したいのかもしれません
It is such a pity that he should feel this way
彼がこのように感じるのはとても残念です
because intelligence is nothing
知性は何もないからです
it is in the heart that the values lie
価値観があるのは心の中にあります

I wish I could make him understand
彼に理解させたい
a loving good heart is riches
愛情深い善良な心は富です
intellect without a good heart is poverty
良い心のない知性は貧困です
Although he talks so little, he has quite a considerable vocabulary
彼はほとんど話しませんが、かなりの語彙を持っています
This morning he used a surprisingly good word
今朝、彼は驚くほど良い言葉を使いました
He evidently recognized that it was a good one
彼は明らかにそれが良いものであることを認識していました
because he made sure to use the word a couple more times
彼はその言葉をあと数回使うようにしたからです
it showed that he possesses a certain quality of perception
それは彼が一定の質の知覚を持っていることを示しました
Without a doubt that seed can be made to grow, if cultivated
栽培すれば、種子を成長させることができることは間違いありません
Where did he get that word?
彼はどこでその言葉を手に入れましたか?
I do not think I have ever used that word
私はその言葉を使ったことがないと思います
No, he took no interest in my name
いいえ、彼は私の名前に興味がありませんでした
I tried to hide my disappointment
私は失望を隠そうとしました
but I suppose I did not succeed
しかし、私は成功しなかったと思います

I went away and sat on the moss-bank
私は立ち去り、苔の土手に座りました
and I put my feet into the water
そして私は足を水に入れました
It is where I go when I hunger for companionship
それは私が交際を渇望するときに行く場所です
when I want someone to look at
誰かに見てもらいたいとき
when I want someone to talk to
誰かに話してもらいたいとき
the lovely white body painted in the pool is not enough
プールに描かれた素敵な白いボディは十分ではありません
but it is something, at least
しかし、それは少なくとも何かです
and something is better than utter loneliness
そして何かが完全な孤独よりも優れています
It talks when I talk
私が話すとき、それは話します

it is sad when I am sad
私が悲しいとき、それは悲しいです
it comforts me with its sympathy
それはその同情で私を慰めます
it says, "Do not be downhearted, you poor friendless girl"
それは、「落胆しないでください、あなたは貧しい友人のない女の子です」と言っています
"I will be your friend"
「私はあなたの友達になります」
It is a good friend to me
それは私にとって良い友達です
it is my only friend and my sister
それは私の唯一の友人であり、私の妹です

I shall never forget first time she forsook me!
彼女が初めて私を見捨てたときのことを私は決して忘れません!
My heart was heavy in my body!
私の心は私の体に重かったです!
I said, "She was all I had"
私は「彼女は私が持っていたすべてでした」と言いました

"and now she is gone!"
「そして今、彼女は去りました!」
In my despair I said "Break, my heart"
絶望の中で私は「壊れて、私の心」と言いました
"I cannot bear my life any more!"
「もう命が耐えられない!」
and I hid my face in my hands
そして私は顔を手で隠しました
and there was no solace for me
そして私には慰めはありませんでした
And when I took my hands away from my face
そして、顔から手を離したとき
and after a little, there she was again
そして少し後、彼女は再びそこにいました
white and shining and beautiful
白く輝く美しい
and I sprang into her arms
そして私は彼女の腕の中に飛び込んだ

That was perfect happiness
それは完璧な幸せでした
I had known happiness before, but it was not like this
私は以前から幸せを知っていましたが、そうではありませんでした
this happiness was ecstasy
この幸せはエクスタシーでした
I never doubted her afterwards
その後、私は彼女を疑うことはありませんでした
Sometimes she stayed away for perhaps an hour
時々彼女はおそらく1時間離れていました
maybe she was gone almost the whole day
多分彼女はほぼ一日中いなくなった
but I waited and I did not doubt her return
しかし、私は待って、彼女が戻ってきたことを疑いませんでした
I said, "She is busy" or "she is gone on a journey"
私は「彼女は忙しい」または「彼女は旅に出ている」と言いました
but I know she will come back, and she always did
しかし、私は彼女が戻ってくることを知っています、そして彼女はいつもそうしました
At night she would not come if it was dark
夜は暗くなければ来ない
because she was a timid little thing
彼女は臆病な小さなものだったので
but if there was a moon she would come
しかし、月があれば彼女は来るでしょう
I am not afraid of the dark
私は暗闇を恐れていません
but she is younger than I am
しかし、彼女は私より若いです
she was born after I was
彼女は私がいた後に生まれました
Many and many are the visits I have paid her
私が彼女に支払った訪問はたくさんあります

she is my comfort and refuge when my life is hard
彼女は私の人生が困難なときの私の慰めと避難所です
and my life is mainly made from hard moments
そして私の人生は主に困難な瞬間から作られています

TUESDAY - 火曜日
All the morning I was at work improving the estate
午前中ずっと私は不動産の改善に取り組んでいました
and I purposely kept away from him
そして私は故意に彼から遠ざかっていました
in the hope that he would get lonely and come
彼が孤独になって来ることを期待して
But he did not come to me
しかし、彼は私のところに来ませんでした
At noon I stopped for the day
正午に私はその日のために立ち止まりました
and I took my recreation
そして私は私のレクリエーションを取りました
I flitted about with the bees and the butterflies
私は蜂と蝶と一緒に飛び回りました
and I revelled in the flowers
そして私は花に夢中になりました
those beautiful happy little creatures
それらの美しい幸せな小さな生き物
they catch the smile of God out of the sky
彼らは空から神の笑顔をキャッチします
and they preserve the smile!
そして彼らは笑顔を保ちます！
I gathered them and made them into wreaths
私はそれらを集めて花輪にしました
and I clothed myself in flowers
そして私は花を着ました
I ate my luncheon; apples
私は昼食を食べました。リンゴ
of course; then I sat in the shade
もちろんです;それから私は日陰に座った
and I wished and waited

そして私は願って待っていました
But he did not come
しかし、彼は来ませんでした

But it is of no loss
しかし、それは損失ではありません
Nothing would have come of it
何も起こらなかったでしょう
because he does not care for flowers
彼は花を気にしないからです
He called them rubbish
彼はそれらをゴミと呼んだ
and he cannot tell one from another
そして彼はお互いを区別することができません

and he thinks it is superior to feel like that
そして彼はそのように感じることが優れていると思います
He does not care for me, flowers
彼は私を気にしません、花
nor does he care for the painted sky in the evening
また、彼は夕方に描かれた空を気にしません
is there anything he does care for?
彼が気にかけていることはありますか?
he cares for nothing except building shacks
彼は小屋を建てる以外は何も気にしません
he builds them to coop himself up
彼は自分自身を協力するためにそれらを構築します
but he's away from the good clean rain
しかし、彼は良いきれいな雨から離れています
and he does not sample the fruits
そして彼は果物を試飲しません

I laid a dry stick on the ground
乾いた棒を地面に置いた
and I tried to bore a hole in it with another one
そして私は別のものでそれに穴を開けようとしました
in order to carry out a scheme that I had
私が持っていた計画を実行するために
and soon I got an awful fright
そしてすぐに私はひどい恐怖を感じました
A thin, transparent bluish film rose out of the hole
薄くて透明な青みがかったフィルムが穴から浮かび上がった
and I dropped everything and ran
そして私はすべてを落として走りました
I thought it was a spirit
精霊だと思いました
and I was so frightened!
そして私はとても怖かったです！
But I looked back and it was not coming;
しかし、私は振り返りました、そしてそれは来ていませんでした。
so I leaned against a rock
だから私は岩にもたれかかった
and I rested and panted
そして私は休んで喘ぎました
and I let my limbs go on trembling
そして私は手足を震わせ続けました
finally they were steady again
ついに彼らは再び安定しました
then I crept warily back
それから私は用心深く忍び寄りました
I was alert, watching, and ready to fly
私は警戒し、見守っていて、飛ぶ準備ができていました
I would run if there was occasion
機会があれば走ります
when I was near I parted the branches of a rose-bush
私が近くにいたとき、私はバラの茂みの枝を分けました
and I peeped through the rose-bush
そして私はバラの茂みをのぞきました

and I wished the man was about
そして私はその男が
I was looking so cunning and pretty
私はとても狡猾できれいに見えました
but the spirit was gone
しかし、精神は消えていました
I went where the spirit was
私は精神があったところに行きました
there was a pinch of delicate pink dust in the hole
穴には繊細なピンクのほこりがつまんでいました
I put my finger in to feel it
私はそれを感じるために指を入れました
and I said "ouch!"
そして私は「痛い!」と言いました。
and I took it out again
そして私はそれを再び取り出しました
It was a cruel pain
それは残酷な痛みでした
I put my finger in my mouth
私は指を口に入れました
I stood on one foot and then the other, grunting
私は片方の足で立ち、次にもう片方の足で立ち、うめき声を上げました
I presently eased my misery
私は今、私の惨めさを和らげました
then I was full of interest and I began to examine
それから私は興味に満ちていて、調べ始めました

I was curious to know what the pink dust was
ピンクのほこりが何であるか知りたいと思いました
Suddenly the name of it occurred to me
突然その名前が浮かびました
I had never heard of it before
聞いたことがなかった
but I knew it was FIRE!
しかし、私はそれが火であることを知っていました!
I was as certain of it
私はそれを確信していました
as certain as a person could be of anything in the world
人が世界の何かである可能性があるのと同じくらい確実です
So without hesitation I named it that — fire
だからためらうことなく私はそれをそれに名付けました—火

I had created something that didn't exist before
私は以前には存在しなかったものを作成しました
I had added a new thing to the world
私は世界に新しいものを追加しました
this world full of uncountable phenomena
数え切れないほどの現象に満ちたこの世界
I realized this and I was proud of my achievement
私はこれに気づき、自分の成果を誇りに思いました
and was going to run and find him
そして走って彼を見つけるつもりでした
I wanted tell him about it
私は彼にそれについて話したかった
I thought it might raise myself in his esteem
彼の尊敬の念が高まりそうだと思いました

but I reflected on it
しかし、私はそれを振り返りました
and I did not do it
そして私はそれをしませんでした
No, he would not care for it
いいえ、彼はそれを気にしません
He would ask what it was good for
彼はそれが何のために良いのか尋ねるでしょう
and what could I answer?
そして私は何に答えることができますか？
it was not good for something, it was merely beautiful
それは何かのために良くありませんでした、それは単に美しかったです

So I sighed, and I did not go
それで私はため息をつきました、そして私は行きませんでした
Because it wasn't good for anything
何の役にも立たなかったからです
it could not build a shack
小屋を建てることができませんでした
it could not improve melon
メロンを改良することはできませんでした
it could not hurry a fruit crop
果物の収穫を急ぐことはできませんでした
it was useless and foolish vanity
それは役に立たず、愚かな虚栄心でした
he would despise it and say cutting words
彼はそれを軽蔑し、言葉を切ると言うでしょう
But to me it was not despicable
しかし、私にとってそれは卑劣ではありませんでした
I said, "Oh, you fire, I love you"
私は「ああ、あなたは発砲します、私はあなたを愛しています」と言いました
"you dainty pink creature, you are BEAUTIFUL"
あなたは可憐なピンクの生き物です、あなたは美しいです
"and being beautiful is enough!"
「そして、美しいことで十分です!」
and I was going to gather it to my breast, but refrained
そして私はそれを私の胸に集めるつもりでしたが、控えました
Then I thought of another maxim
それから私は別の格言を考えました
it was very similar to the first one
それは最初のものと非常に似ていました
I was afraid it was a plagiarism
盗作ではないかと心配しました
"THE BURNT EXPERIMENT SHUNS THE FIRE"
「焼けた実験は火を避けます」
I repeated my experiment
私は実験を繰り返しました

I had made a good deal of fire-dust
私はかなりの火のほこりを作りました
and I emptied it into a handful of dry brown grass
そして私はそれを一握りの乾いた茶色の草に空にしました
I was intending to carry it home
私はそれを家に持ち帰るつもりでした
and I wanted to keep it and play with it
そして私はそれを維持し、それで遊びたかった
but the wind struck it and it sprayed up
しかし、風がそれを襲い、それはスプレーしました
and it spat out at me fiercely
そしてそれは私に激しく吐き出しました
and I dropped it and ran
そして私はそれを落として走りました
When I looked back the blue spirit was towering up
振り返ると、青い精霊がそびえ立っていました
and it was stretching and rolling away like a cloud
そしてそれは雲のように伸びて転がっていました
and instantly I thought of the name of it — SMOKE!
そしてすぐに私はそれの名前を考えました—スモーク！
and upon my word, I had never heard of smoke before
そして私の言葉で、私はこれまで煙について聞いたことがありませんでした

Soon brilliant yellow and red flares shot up
すぐに鮮やかな黄色と赤のフレアが飛び上がりました
they shot up through the smoke
彼らは煙の中を飛び上がった
and I named them in an instant — FLAMES
そして私はすぐにそれらに名前を付けました—炎
and I was right about this too
そしてこれについても正しかった
even though these were the very first flames there had ever been
これらは今までに起こった最初の炎でしたが
They climbed the trees and they flashed splendidly
彼らは木に登り、見事に点滅しました
there was increasing volume of tumbling smoke
転がる煙の量が増えていました
and the flames danced in and out of the smoke
そして炎は煙の中を出入りしました
and I had to clap my hands and laugh and dance
そして私は手をたたき、笑い、踊らなければなりませんでした
it was so new and strange
それはとても新しくて奇妙でした
and it was so wonderful and beautiful!
そして、それはとても素晴らしくて美しかったです!

He came running, and he stopped and gazed
彼は走って来て、立ち止まって見つめました
he said not a word for many minutes
彼は何分も一言も言わなかった
Then he asked what it was
それから彼はそれが何であるか尋ねました
it a shame he asked such a direct question
彼がそのような直接的な質問をしたのは残念でした
I had to answer it, of course, and I did
もちろん、私はそれに答えなければなりませんでした、そして私はそうしました
if it annoyed him, what could I do?
それが彼を苛立たせたなら、私は何ができますか?
it's not my fault that I knew what it was

それが何であるかを知っていたのは私のせいではありません
I said it was fire
私はそれが火事だと言った
I had no desire to annoy him
私は彼を困らせるつもりはありませんでした
After a pause he asked: "How did it come?"
少し間を置いた後、彼は尋ねました:「それはどうやって来たのですか?」
this question also had to have a direct answer
この質問にも直接答えが必要でした
"I made it" I answered
「やった」と私は答えた
The fire was travelling farther and farther away
火はどんどん遠ざかっていました
He went to the edge of the burned place
彼は焼けた場所の端に行きました
and he stood looking down at it
そして彼はそれを見下ろして立っていました
and he said: "What are these?"
そして彼は言った:「これらは何ですか?」
I told him they were fire-coals
私は彼に彼らが火炭であると言いました
He picked up one to examine it
彼はそれを調べるためにそれを拾いました
but he changed his mind and put it down again
しかし、彼は考えを変えて、それを再び置きました
Then he went away
それから彼は去りました
NOTHING interests him
彼には何も興味がありません

But I was interested
しかし、私は興味がありました
There were ashes, gray and soft and delicate and pretty
灰があり、灰色で柔らかく、繊細できれいでした
I knew what they were straight away
私は彼らが何であるかをすぐに知った
And the embers; I knew the embers, too
そして残り火;残り火も知っていました
I found my apples and I raked them out
私は自分のリンゴを見つけて、それらをかき集めました
and I was glad because I am very young
そして私はとても若いのでうれしかったです
so my appetite is still very active
だから私の食欲はまだ非常に活発です

But I was disappointed by the experiment
しかし、私は実験に失望しました
because all the apples were burst open and spoiled
すべてのリンゴが破裂して甘やかされていたからです
at least, I thought they were spoiled
少なくとも、私は彼らが甘やかされていると思いました
but they were not actually spoiled
しかし、彼らは実際には甘やかされていませんでした
they were better than raw ones
彼らは生のものよりも優れていました
Fire is beautiful and some day it will be useful, I think
火は美しく、いつか役に立つと思います

FRIDAY - 金曜日

I saw him again, for a moment
私は一瞬、彼に再び会った
last Monday at nightfall, but only for a moment
先週の月曜日の日暮れですが、ほんの一瞬です
I was hoping he would praise me for trying to improve the estate
私は彼が不動産を改善しようとしたことで私を賞賛することを望んでいました
because I had meant well and had worked hard
私は善意があり、一生懸命働いていたからです
But he was not pleased and he turned away and left me
しかし、彼は喜ばず、背を向けて私を去りました
He was also displeased on another account
彼はまた別のアカウントで不快でした
I tried to persuade him to stop going over the water falls
私は彼に滝を越えるのをやめるように説得しようとしました
the fire had revealed to me a new feeling
火事は私に新しい気持ちを明らかにしました
this feeling was quite new
この感覚はかなり新鮮でした
it felt distinctly different from love or grief
それは愛や悲しみとは明らかに違うと感じました
and it was different from the other passions I had discovered
そしてそれは私が発見した他の情熱とは異なっていました
this new feeling was FEAR and it is horrible!
この新しい感覚は恐怖であり、それは恐ろしいです!
I wish I had never discovered it
私はそれを発見しなかったらよかったのに
it gives me dark moments and spoils my happiness
それは私に暗い瞬間を与え、私の幸せを台無しにします
it makes me shiver and tremble and shudder
それは私を震えさせ、震えさせ、震えさせます
But I could not persuade him
しかし、私は彼を説得することができませんでした
he has not discovered fear yet
彼はまだ恐怖を発見していません

so he could not understand me
だから彼は私を理解できませんでした

- Extract from Adam's Diary -
-アダムの日記からの抜粋-

Perhaps I ought to remember that she is very young
おそらく私は彼女がとても若いことを覚えておくべきです
she is still but a mere girl
彼女はまだただの女の子です
and I should make allowances
そして私は手当をするべきです
She is all interest, eagerness, vivacity

彼女はすべて興味、熱意、活力です
she finds the world endlessly charming
彼女は世界が際限なく魅力的だと感じています
a wonder, a mystery, a joy
不思議、謎、喜び
she can't speak for delight when she finds a new flower
彼女は新しい花を見つけたとき、喜びについて話すことができません
she must pet it and caress it
彼女はそれを撫でて愛撫しなければなりません
and she has to smell it and talk to it
そして彼女はそれを嗅ぎ、それと話さなければなりません
and she pours out endearing names upon it
そして彼女はそれに愛らしい名前を注ぎます
And she is color-mad; brown rocks, yellow sand
そして彼女は色に狂っています。茶色の岩、黄色い砂
gray moss, green foliage, blue sky, the pearl of the dawn
灰色の苔、緑の葉、青い空、夜明けの真珠
the purple shadows on the mountains
山の上の紫色の影
the golden islands floating in crimson seas at sunset
夕暮れ時に真紅の海に浮かぶ黄金の島々
the pallid moon sailing through the shredded cloud-rack
細断された雲棚を航行する淡い月
the star-jewels glittering in the wastes of space
宇宙の荒れ地にきらめく星の宝石
none of these names are of any practical value
これらの名前はどれも実用的な価値はありません
there's no value in them as far as I can see
私が見る限り、それらには価値がありません
but they have color and majesty
しかし、彼らは色と威厳を持っています
and that is enough for her
そしてそれは彼女にとって十分です
and she loses her mind over them
そして彼女はそれらについて彼女の心を失います
If only she could quiet down a little

彼女が少し静かにすることができれば
I wish she kept still a couple minutes at a time
彼女が一度に数分じっとしていたらいいのにと思います
it would be a reposeful spectacle
それは安らぎの光景になるでしょう
In that case I think I could enjoy looking at her
その場合は、彼女を見るのが楽しくできたと思います
indeed, I am sure I could enjoy her company
確かに、私は彼女の会社を楽しむことができたと確信しています
I am coming to realize that she is a quite remarkable creature
私は彼女が非常に注目に値する生き物であることに気づき始めています
lithe, slender, trim, rounded
しなやか, 細身, トリム, 丸みを帯びた
shapely, nimble, graceful
格好良く、軽快で、優雅
and once she was standing as white as marble
そしてかつて彼女は大理石のように白く立っていました
she was on a boulder, and drenched in the sun
彼女は岩の上にいて、太陽の下でびしょ濡れでした
she stood with her young head tilted back
彼女は若い頭を後ろに傾けて立っていた
and her hand was shading her eyes
そして彼女の手は彼女の目を覆い隠していた
she was watching the flight of a bird in the sky
彼女は空を飛ぶ鳥の飛翔を見ていた
I recognized that she was beautiful
私は彼女が美しいことを認識しました

MONDAY NOON - 月曜日の正午

Is there anything that she is not interested in?
彼女が興味を持っていないことはありますか?
if there is something, it is not in my list
何かがあれば、それは私のリストにありません
There are animals that I am indifferent to
私が無関心な動物がいます
but it is not so with her
しかし、それは彼女には当てはまりません
She has no discrimination
彼女には差別はありません
she takes to all the animals
彼女はすべての動物に連れて行きます
she thinks they are all treasures
彼女はそれらがすべて宝物だと思っています
every new animal is welcome
すべての新しい動物は大歓迎です

take the mighty brontosaurus as an example
例として強力なブロントサウルスを取り上げます
she regarded it as an acquisition
彼女はそれを買収と見なしました
I considered it a calamity
私はそれを災難だと思った
that is a good sample of the lack of harmony
それは調和の欠如の良いサンプルです
a lack of harmony between our views of things
物事に対する私たちの見方の間の調和の欠如
She wanted to domesticate it
彼女はそれを飼いならしたかった
I wanted to give it the house and move out
家を譲って引っ越したかった
She believed it could be tamed by kind treatment
彼女はそれが親切な扱いによって飼いならされると信じていました
and she thought it would be a good pet
そして彼女はそれが良いペットになると思った
I tried to convince her otherwise

私は別の方法で彼女を説得しようとしました
a pet twenty-one feet high is no thing to have at home
高さ21フィートのペットは家に飼うものではありません
even with the best intentions it could sit down on the house
最善の意図があっても、それは家に座ることができます
it wouldn't have to mean any harm
それは害を意味する必要はありません
but it could still mash the house quite easily
しかし、それはまだ家を非常に簡単に粉砕することができます
for anyone could see that it was absent-minded
誰もがそれがぼんやりしていることを見ることができたからです
because it had an emptiness behind its eyes
目の後ろに空虚さがあったからです
Still, her heart was set upon having that monster
それでも、彼女の心はその怪物を持つことに決心していました
and she couldn't give it up
そして彼女はそれをあきらめることができませんでした
She thought we could start a dairy with it
彼女は私たちがそれで乳製品を始めることができると思った
and she wanted me to help milk it
そして彼女は私にそれを搾乳するのを手伝ってほしかった
but I wouldn't milk it
しかし、私はそれを搾乳しません
it was too risky
リスクが高すぎました
The sex wasn't right for milking either
セックスも搾乳に適していませんでした
and we didn't have a ladder anyway
とにかくはしごがありませんでした
Then she wanted to ride it
それから彼女はそれに乗ってみたかった
she thought she would get a better view of the scenery
彼女は景色がよく見えると思った
Thirty or forty feet of its tail was lying on the ground

その尾の30フィートか40フィートが地面に横たわっていました
it had all the size of a fallen tree
倒木ほどの大きさでした
and she thought she could climb it
そして彼女はそれを登ることができると思った
but she was mistaken
しかし、彼女は間違っていました
when she got to the steep place it was too slick
彼女が急な場所に着いたとき、それはあまりにも滑らかでした
and she came sliding back down
そして彼女は滑り落ちてきました
she would have hurt herself if it wasn't for me
それが私のためでなければ、彼女は自分自身を傷つけていただろう

Was she satisfied now? No
彼女は今満足しましたか?いいえ
Nothing ever satisfies her but demonstration
デモンストレーション以外に彼女を満足させるものはありません
she didn't keep theories untested for long
彼女は長い間理論をテストしなかった
It is the right spirit, I concede
それは正しい精神です、私は認めます
it is what attracts me to her
それが私を彼女に引き付けるものです
I feel the influence of it
その影響を感じます
if I were with her more I think I would become more adventurous
彼女ともっと一緒にいたら、もっと冒険的になると思います
Well, she had one theory remaining about this colossus
さて、彼女はこの巨像について1つの理論を残していました
she thought that if we could tame it we could stand in the river
彼女は、飼いならすことができれば川に立つことができると考えました
if we made him our friend we could use him as a bridge
彼を友達にすれば、彼を架け橋として使うことができます
It turned out that he was already plenty tame enough
彼はすでに十分に飼いならされていたことがわかりました
he was tame enough as far as she was concerned
彼女に関する限り、彼は十分に飼いならされていました
so she tried her theory, but it failed
それで彼女は自分の理論を試しましたが、失敗しました
she got him properly placed in the river
彼女は彼を川に適切に配置しました
and she went ashore to cross over him
そして彼女は彼を横切るために上陸した
but he came out and followed her around
しかし、彼は出てきて彼女を追いかけました
like a pet mountain

ペットの山のように
Like the other animals
他の動物のように
They all do that
彼らは皆それをします

- Eve's Diary -
- イブの日記 –

Tuesday, Wednesday, Thursday, and today:
火曜日、水曜日、木曜日、および今日：
I didn't see him any of these days
私は最近彼に会っていませんでした
It is a long time to be alone
一人でいるのは長い時間です
still, it is better to be alone than unwelcome
それでも、歓迎されないよりも一人でいる方が良いです
FRIDAY
金曜日
I HAD to have company
私は会社を持たなければなりませんでした
I was made for having company, I think
私は会社を持つために作られたと思います
so I made friends with the animals
だから私は動物と友達になりました
They are just so charming
彼らはとても魅力的です
and they have the kindest disposition
そして彼らは最も親切な気質を持っています
and they have the politest ways
そして彼らは最も丁寧な方法を持っています
they never look sour or let you feel that you are intruding
彼らは決して酸っぱく見えたり、あなたが侵入していると感じさせたりすることはありません
they smile at you and wag their tail
彼らはあなたに微笑んで尻尾を振る
at least, they wag their tale if they've got one
少なくとも、彼らがそれを持っているなら、彼らは彼らの物語を振る
and they are always ready for a romp or an excursion
そして、彼らはいつでも暴れや遠足の準備ができています
they're ready for anything you want to propose
彼らはあなたが提案したいことは何でも準備ができています

I think they are perfect gentlemen
彼らは完璧な紳士だと思います
All these days we have had such good times
最近、私たちはとても楽しい時間を過ごしました
and it hasn't been lonesome for me, ever
そして、それは私にとって決して孤独ではありませんでした

Lonesome? No, I should say not
寂しい！いいえ、そうではないと言うべきです
there's always a swarm of them around
周りには常にそれらの群れがあります
sometimes as much as four or five acres
時には4〜5エーカーも
when you stand on a rock you can see them for miles
あなたが岩の上に立つとき、あなたはそれらを何マイルも見ることができます
they are mottled and splashed and gay with color

彼らはまだらで、はねかけられ、色で同性愛者です
and there's a frisking sheen and sun-flash
そして、フリスクのある光沢と太陽の閃光があります
and the landscape is so rippled with stripes
そして風景は縞模様でとても波打っています
you might think it was a lake
湖だと思うかもしれません
but you know it isn't a lake at all
しかし、あなたはそれがまったく湖ではないことを知っています
and there are storms of sociable birds
そして社交的な鳥の嵐があります
and there are hurricanes of whirring wings
そして、旋回する翼のハリケーンがあります
and the sun strikes all that feathery commotion
そして太陽はそのすべての羽毛のような騒ぎを打ちます
you can see a blazing up of all the colors you can think of
あなたはあなたが考えることができるすべての色の燃え上がるのを見ることができます
enough colours to put your eyes out
目を出すのに十分な色

We have made long excursions
私たちは長い遠足をしました
and I have seen a great deal of the world
そして私は世界をたくさん見てきました
I think I've seen almost all of it
私はそれのほとんどすべてを見たと思います
I must be first traveler
私は最初の旅行者でなければなりません
and I am the only traveller
そして私は唯一の旅行者です
When we are on the march, it is an imposing sight
私たちが行進しているとき、それは印象的な光景です
there's nothing like it anywhere
そのようなものはどこにもありません
For comfort I ride a tiger or a leopard
快適さのために私はトラやヒョウに乗る
because they are soft and have round backs that fit me
彼らは柔らかく、私に合う丸い背中を持っているからです
and because they are such pretty animals
そして彼らはとてもかわいい動物だからです
but for long distance, or for scenery, I ride the elephant
しかし、長距離や風景のために、私は象に乗ります
He hoists me up with his trunk
彼はトランクで私を持ち上げます
but I can get off myself
しかし、私は自分自身を降りることができます
when we are ready to camp he sits
私たちがキャンプする準備ができたら、彼は座っています
and I slide down off his back
そして私は彼の背中から滑り落ちます

The birds and animals are all friendly to each other
鳥や動物はすべてお互いに友好的です
and there are no disputes about anything
そして、何についても論争はありません
They all talk with each other and to me
彼らは皆、お互いに、そして私に話しかけます
but it must be a foreign language
しかし、それは外国語でなければなりません
because I cannot make out a word they say
彼らが言う言葉がわからないからです
yet they often understand me when I talk back
それでも、私が話し返すとき、彼らはしばしば私を理解します
the dog and the elephant understand me particularly well

犬と象は私を特によく理解しています
It makes me ashamed
それは私を恥ずかしく思います
It shows that they are more intelligent than I am
それは彼らが私よりも賢いことを示しています
but I want to be the main experiment
しかし、私は主な実験になりたいです
and I intend to be the main experiment
そして私は主な実験になるつもりです
I have learned a number of things
私は多くのことを学びました
and I am educated, now
そして私は今教育を受けています
but I wasn't educated at first
しかし、私は最初は教育を受けていませんでした
I was ignorant at first
私は最初は無知でした
At first it used to vex me
最初は私をベックスしていました
because I was never smart enough
私は決して賢くなかったからです
I wasn't smart enough despite how much I observed
どれだけ観察しても、私は十分に賢くありませんでした
I was never around when the water was running uphill
水が上り坂を流れているとき、私は周りにいませんでした
but now I do not mind it
しかし今私はそれを気にしません
I have experimented and experimented
私は実験し、実験しました
I know it never runs uphill, except in the dark
暗闇の中を除いて、それが上り坂を走ることは決してないことを私は知っています
I know it does run uphill when it is dark
暗いときは上り坂を走ることは知っています
because the pool never goes dry
プールが乾くことはないからです
it would dry up if the water didn't come back in the night

夜に水が戻ってこないと乾きます
It is best to prove things by actual experiment
実際の実験で証明するのが一番です
if you do an experiment then you KNOW
あなたが実験をするなら、あなたは知っています
whereas if you depend on guessing you never get educated
一方、推測に依存している場合、教育を受けることはありません

thinking about things is not enough either
物事を考えるだけでは十分ではありません
Some things you CAN'T find out
あなたが見つけることができないいくつかのこと
but you will never know you can't by guessing and supposing:
しかし、あなたは推測して仮定することによってあなたがで

きないことを決して知りません:
no, you have to be patient and go on experimenting
いいえ、辛抱強く実験を続ける必要があります
until you find out that you can't find out
あなたが見つけることができないことを知るまで
And it is delightful to have it that way
そして、それをそのようにすることは楽しいことです
it makes the world so interesting
それは世界をとても面白くします
If there wasn't anything to find out, it would be dull
調べるものが何もなければ、それは鈍いでしょう
Even not finding out is just as interesting
見つけなくても同じくらい面白いです
sometimes not finding out is as interesting as finding out
時々見つけないことは見つけることと同じくらい面白いです
The secret of the water was a treasure until I got it
水の秘密は手に入れるまで宝物でした
then the excitement all went away
その後、興奮はすべて消えました
and I recognized a sense of loss
そして私は喪失感を認識しました

By experiment I know that wood swims
実験によって、私は木が泳ぐことを知っています
dry leaves, feathers, and other things float too
乾燥した葉、羽、その他のものも浮かんでいます
so you can know that a rock can swim
だからあなたは岩が泳ぐことができることを知ることができます
because you've collected cumulative evidence
累積的な証拠を集めたからです
but you have to put up with simply knowing it
しかし、あなたは単にそれを知ることに我慢しなければなりません
because there isn't any way to prove it
それを証明する方法がないからです
at least up until now there's no way to prove it
少なくとも今まではそれを証明する方法はありません
But I shall find a way
しかし、私は方法を見つけるでしょう
then that excitement will go
その後、その興奮は行きます
Such things make me sad
そのようなことは私を悲しくさせます
by and by I will come to know everything
やがて私はすべてを知るようになるでしょう
and then there won't be any more excitement
そして、これ以上の興奮はありません
and I do love excitements so much!
そして私は興奮がとても好きです!
The other night I couldn't sleep
先日の夜、私は眠れませんでした
I was thinking so much about it
私はそれについてとても考えていました

At first I couldn't establish what I was made for
最初は、自分が何のために作られたのかを確立できませんでした

but now I think I know what I was made for
しかし今、私は自分が何のために作られたのかを知っていると思います

I was made to search out the secrets of this wonderful world
この素晴らしい世界の秘密を探させられました

and I am made to be happy
そして私は幸せになるように作られています

I think the Giver of it all for devising it
私はそれを考案するためのすべての贈与者だと思います

I think there are still many things to learn
まだまだ学ぶべきことはたくさんあると思います

and I hope there will always be more to learn
そして私は常に学ぶべきことがもっとあることを願っています
by not hurrying too fast I think they will last weeks and weeks
あまり速く急がないことで、彼らは数週間と数週間続くと思います
I hope I have so much left to discover
発見することがたくさん残っていることを願っています
When you cast up a feather it sails away on the air
あなたが羽を投げると、それは空中を航海します
and then it goes out of sight
そしてそれは見えなくなります
when you throw up a clod it doesn't act like a feather
あなたが塊を投げるとき、それは羽のようには機能しません
It comes down, every time
毎回降りてきます
I have tried it and tried it
私はそれを試して試しました
and it is always this way
そしてそれはいつもこのようです
I wonder why it is
なんでだろう
Of course it DOESN'T come down
もちろん、それは降りません
but why does it SEEM to come down?
しかし、なぜそれが下がっているように見えるのですか?
I suppose it is an optical illusion
目の錯覚だと思います
I mean, one of them is an optical illusion
つまり、そのうちの1つは目の錯覚です
I don't know which one is an optical illusion
どれが目の錯覚なのかわかりません
It may be the feather, it may be the clod
それは羽かもしれません、それは塊かもしれません
I can't prove which it is
私はそれがどれであるかを証明することはできません

I can only demonstrate that one or the other is a fake
どちらかが偽物であることを示すことしかできません
and I let you take your choice
そして私はあなたにあなたの選択をさせます

By watching, I know that the stars are not going to last
見ていると、星は長続きしないことがわかります
I have seen some of the best ones melt
私は最高のもののいくつかが溶けるのを見てきました
and then they ran down the sky
そして彼らは空を駆け下りた
Since one can melt, they can all melt
1つは溶けることができるので、それらはすべて溶けることができます

since they can all melt, they can all melt the same night
それらはすべて溶けることができるので、それらはすべて同じ夜に溶けることができます

That sorrow will come, I know it
その悲しみは来るでしょう、私はそれを知っています

I mean to sit up every night and look at them
私は毎晩起きてそれらを見ることを意味します

as long as I can keep awake
目を覚まし続けることができる限り

and I will impress those sparkling fields on my memory
そして私はそれらのきらめくフィールドを私の記憶に印象づけます

so that I can by my fancy restore those lovely myriads
私の空想によってそれらの素敵な無数を復元することができるように

then I can put them back into the black sky, when they are taken away
それから私は彼らが連れ去られたとき、彼らを黒い空に戻すことができます

and I can make them sparkle again
そして私はそれらを再び輝かせることができます

and I can double them by the blur of my tears
そして私は私の涙のぼかしによってそれらを倍増させることができます

- After the Fall -
- 秋の後 -

When I look back, the Garden is a dream to me
振り返ってみると、庭は私にとって夢です
It was beautiful, surpassingly beautiful, enchantingly beautiful
それは美しく、非常に美しく、魅惑的に美しかった
and now the garden is lost
そして今、庭は失われています
and I shall not see it any more
そして私はそれをもう見ないでしょう

The Garden is lost, but I have found him
庭は失われましたが、私は彼を見つけました
and I am content with that
そして私はそれに満足しています
He loves me as well as he can
彼はできる限り私を愛しています
I love him with all the strength of my passionate nature
私は私の情熱的な性質のすべての強さで彼を愛しています
and this is proper to my youth and sex, I think
そしてこれは私の若さと性別にふさわしいと思います
If I ask myself why I love him, I find I do not know
なぜ彼を愛しているのかと自問すると、わかりません
and I do not really care to know
そして私は本当に知る気にしません
so I suppose this kind of love is not a product of reasoning
ですから、この種の愛は推論の産物ではないと思います
this love has nothing to do with statistics
この愛は統計とは何の関係もありません
it is different to the way one loves the animals
それは動物を愛する方法とは異なります
I think that this must be so
これはそうに違いないと思います
I love certain birds because of their song
私は彼らの歌のために特定の鳥が大好きです
but I do not love Adam on account of his singing
しかし、私は彼の歌のためにアダムを愛していません
No, it is not that
いいえ、そうではありません
the more he sings the more I do not get reconciled to it
彼が歌えば歌うほど、私はそれに和解しません
Yet I ask him to sing
それでも私は彼に歌うように頼みます
because I wish to learn to like everything he is interested in
彼が興味を持っているものすべてを好きになることを学びたいからです
I am sure I can learn

私は学ぶことができると確信しています
because at first I could not stand it, but now I can
最初は我慢できなかったので、今は我慢できます
It sours the milk, but it doesn't matter
それはミルクを酸っぱいしますが、それは問題ではありません
I can get used to that kind of milk
私はそのようなミルクに慣れることができます

It is not on account of his brightness that I love him
私が彼を愛しているのは彼の明るさのせいではありません
no, it is not that
いいえ、そうではありません
He is not to blame for his brightness
彼は彼の明るさのせいではありません
because he did not make it himself
彼は自分でそれをしなかったので
he is as God made him
彼は神が彼を造られた通りです
and that is sufficient the way he is
そして、それは彼のやり方で十分です
There was a wise purpose in it, that I know
そこには賢明な目的がありました
In time the purpose will develop
やがて目的は発展するでしょう
though I think it will not be sudden
突然ではないと思いますが
and besides, there is no hurry
その上、急いではありません
he is good enough just as he is
彼はそのままで十分です
It is not his grace for which I love him
私が彼を愛しているのは彼の恵みではありません
and I do not love him for his delicate nature
そして私は彼の繊細な性質のために彼を愛していません
he would not be considerate for love either
彼も愛に配慮しないでしょう
No, he is lacking in these regards
いいえ、彼はこれらの点で欠けています
but he is well enough just as he is
しかし、彼は彼と同じように十分に元気です
and he is improving
そして彼は改善しています

It is not on account of his industry that I love him
私が彼を愛しているのは彼の業界のせいではありません
No, it is not that
いいえ、そうではありません
I think he has it in him
彼は彼の中にそれを持っていると思います
and I do not know why he conceals it from me
そしてなぜ彼がそれを私から隠しているのかわかりません
It is my only pain
それが私の唯一の痛みです
Otherwise he is frank and open with me, now
そうでなければ、彼は率直で、今は私に対してオープンです
I am sure he keeps nothing from me but this
彼は私から何も守っていないと確信していますが、これ

It grieves me that he should have a secret from me
彼が私から秘密を持っているべきだと私は悲しんでいます
and sometimes it spoils my sleep thinking of it
そして時々それはそれを考えると私の睡眠を台無しにします
but I will put it out of my mind
しかし、私はそれを私の心の外に置きます
it shall not trouble my happiness
それは私の幸せを悩ませることはありません
my happiness is already almost overflowing
私の幸せはすでにほとんど溢れています
It is not on account of his education that I love him
私が彼を愛しているのは彼の教育のせいではありません
No, it is not that
いいえ、そうではありません
He is self-educated
彼は独学です
and he does really know a multitude of things
そして彼は本当に多くのことを知っています
It is not on account of his chivalry that I love him
私が彼を愛しているのは彼の騎士道のせいではありません
No, it is not that
いいえ、そうではありません
He told on me, but I do not blame him
彼は私に言ったが、私は彼を責めない
it is a peculiarity of sex, I think
それはセックスの特殊性だと思います
and he did not make his sex
そして彼は彼のセックスをしませんでした
Of course I would not have told on him
もちろん、私は彼に話さなかっただろう
I would have perished before telling on him
私は彼に話す前に死んでいたでしょう
but that is a peculiarity of sex, too
しかし、それもセックスの特殊性です
and I do not take credit for it
そして私はそれを信用しません
because I did not make my sex

私はセックスをしなかったので
Then why is it that I love him?
では、なぜ私は彼を愛しているのですか?
MERELY BECAUSE HE IS MASCULINE, I think
彼が男性的だから、私は思います

At bottom he is good, and I love him for that
根底で彼は良いです、そして私はそれのために彼を愛しています

but I could love him without him being good
しかし、私は彼が良くなくても彼を愛することができました
If he beat me and abused me I could go on loving him
彼が私を殴り、虐待した場合、私は彼を愛し続けることができます
I know it is that way
私はそれがそうであることを知っています
It is a matter of my sex, I think
それは私の性別の問題だと思います
He is strong and handsome
彼は強くてハンサムです
and I love him for that
そして私はそのために彼を愛しています
and I admire him
そして私は彼を尊敬しています
and am proud of him
そして彼を誇りに思っています
but I could love him without those qualities
しかし、私はそれらの資質なしで彼を愛することができました
If he were plain, I would still love him
彼が地味だったら、私はまだ彼を愛しているでしょう
if he were a wreck, I would still love him
彼が難破船だったら、私はまだ彼を愛しているでしょう
and I would work for him
そして私は彼のために働くでしょう
and I would slave over him
そして私は彼を奴隷にするでしょう
and I would pray for him
そして私は彼のために祈ります
and I would watch by his bedside until I died
そして私は死ぬまで彼のベッドサイドで見守っていました

Yes, I think I love him merely because he is MINE
はい、私は彼が私のものであるという理由だけで彼を愛しているとおもいます
and I love him because he is MASCULINE
そして彼は男性的だから私は彼を愛しています
There is no other reason, I suppose
他に理由はないと思います
And so I think it is as I first said
そして、それは私が最初に言った通りだと思います
this kind of love is not a product of reasoning and statistics
この種の愛は、推論や統計の産物ではありません
this kind of love just comes by itself
この種の愛はそれ自体でやって来ます
No one knows when it will come

それがいつ来るかは誰にもわかりません
and love cannot explain itself
そして愛はそれ自体を説明することはできません
love doesn't need to explain itself
愛はそれ自体を説明する必要はありません
that is what I think, but I am only a girl
そう思いますが、私はただの女の子です
I am the first girl that has examined this matter
私はこの問題を調べた最初の女の子です
although, out of inexperience, I may not have gotten it right
経験不足から、私はそれを正しく理解できなかったかもしれませんが

- Forty Years Later -
-40年後-

It is my prayer, it is my longing;
それは私の祈りであり、私の憧れです。
I pray that we pass from this life together
私たちが一緒にこの人生から過ぎ去ることを祈ります
this longing shall never perish from the earth
この憧れは、決して地上から滅びることはありません
but it shall have place in the heart of every wife that loves
しかし、それは愛するすべての妻の心の中にあるでしょう
until the end of time
時間の終わりまで
and it shall be called by my name; Eve
そしてそれはわたしの名で呼ばれるであろう。イブ

But if one of us must go first, it is my prayer that it shall be I
しかし、私たちの一人が最初に行かなければならない場合、それは私であることが私の祈りです
for he is strong, I am weak
彼は強いので、私は弱いです
I am not as necessary to him as he is to me
私は彼にとって、彼が私にとってそうであるほど必要ではありません
life without him would not be life
彼なしでの人生は人生ではないでしょう
how could I endure it?
どうすればそれに耐えることができますか?
This prayer is also immortal
この祈りも不滅です
this prayer will not cease from being offered up while my race continues
この祈りは、私のレースが続く間、捧げられるのをやめません
I am the first wife
私は最初の妻です
and in the last wife I shall be repeated
そして最後の妻で私は繰り返されるでしょう

- At Eve's Grave -
-イブの墓で-

ADAM: "Wheresoever she was, there was Eden"
アダム:「彼女がどこにいても、エデンがいました」

www.ingramcontent.com/pod-product-compliance
Lightning Source LLC
Chambersburg PA
CBHW011952090526
44591CB00020B/2733